PEARLS & PEBBLES

Catharine Parr Traill

PEARLS & PEBBLES

Edited by
Elizabeth Thompson

NATURAL HERITAGE BOOKS
TORONTO

Published by Natural Heritage/Natural History Inc.
P.O. Box 95, Station O, Toronto, Ontario M4A 2M8

Frontispiece: "Yours Very Sincerely, Catharine Parr Traill,"
from *Pearls and Pebbles* (1894).
Back cover photo: Catharine Parr Traill (1802–1899) with two of
her granddaughters, Ston[e]y Lake, Ontario, Circa 1850.

Design by Blanche Hamill, Norton Hamill Design
Printed and bound in Canada by Hignell Printing Limited

Canadian Cataloguing in Publication Data

Traill, Catherine Parr, 1802–1899
Pearls and pebbles

Includes bibliographical references and index.
ISBN 1-896219-59-4

1. Natural history—Ontario. I., Thompson, Elizabeth Helen, 1952–
II. title.

QH81.T82 1999   508.71   C99-931716-4

THE CANADA COUNCIL | LE CONSEIL DES ARTS
FOR THE ARTS | DU CANADA
SINCE 1957 | DEPUIS 1957

Natural Heritage/Natural History Inc. acknowledges the support received for its publishing program from the Canada Council Block Grant Program. We also acknowledge with
gratitude the assistance of the Association for the Export of Canadian Books, Ottawa.

*This book is dedicated to Margaret Phyllis Thompson:
writer, researcher, and colleague.*

ACKNOWLEDGMENTS

I would like to thank Karen Kingsmill for her research assistance and for her encouragement.

CONTENTS

EDITOR'S INTRODUCTION

ABOUT THE AUTHOR, CATHARINE PARR TRAILL

CATHARINE Parr (Strickland) Traill was born in England in 1802, and grew up in Suffolk. She was the fifth of eight children in a middle-class family—several of whom became well-known writers, two examples being Agnes Strickland, *Lives of the Queens of England* (1840–1848) and Susanna Moodie, *Roughing It in the Bush* (1852) Catharine began writing while she was very young, publishing *The Tell Tale: An Original Collection of Moral and Amusing Stories* (1818) when she was only sixteen. During her teens and twenties, Catharine continued to write: moral children's tales, books about nature and natural history, as well as poems and sketches that she contributed to English periodicals. Her family, left in a precarious financial position by the death of Catharine's father, Thomas Strickland, in 1818, welcomed her assistance, meager though it might be.

In May 1832 Catharine married Thomas Traill, a half-pay officer in the British army. Deciding that they could not support a family on his income, and hoping for improved circumstances in the New World, in July 1832, the couple set sail for Upper Canada (now Ontario). Like many middle-class English emigrants, the Traills were unprepared, mentally or physically, for backwoods life and encountered countless unforeseen difficulties. Although the anticipated prosperity never materialized, as a writer, Catharine Traill capitalized on her pioneer experiences, publishing such non-fiction Canadian classics as *The Backwoods of Canada* (1836) and *The Canadian Settler's Guide* (1854); lively and pragmatic, these books were popular at the time and are still widely-read today.

Catharine Traill's life in Canada affected her fiction as well, for in Catherine Maxwell, the protagonist of *Canadian Crusoes* (1852), she creates the prototype for a heroine who can be found in Canadian fiction up to and including the present: a practical, capable pioneer woman who survives, even thrives on a hostile frontier. Traill's definition of the ideal frontiers woman represents a significant contribution to Canadian literature.

An inveterate scribbler, Traill was still writing when she was in her nineties, publishing *Pearls and Pebbles* in 1894 and *Cot and Cradle Stories* in 1895. *Pearls and Pebbles* represents a culmination of sorts, for in it Traill has collected sketches written throughout her life, featuring, but not limited to her knowledge of Canada. Near the end of the century, and almost a century old herself, Traill looks back to reflect on her life and on Canadian pioneering; she looks around her and observes her contemporary landscape; and she looks ahead to the twentieth century, predicting further changes in the place she loves.

Nor was Traill finished here. *Cot and Cradle Stories*, a collection of children's stories, appeared the following year, and as her journals make clear,[1] she had further work in mind. Her pen was stilled only by her death in 1899—but through her lively and timeless writing, the spirit of the woman lives on.

ABOUT THE BOOK

It is hard to believe that Catharine Traill's *Pearls and Pebbles* was published over one hundred years ago, for its captivating charm goes beyond one particular time and place; indeed it reaches out to us today with undiminished vigour. While a good deal of the book's *joie de vivre* stems from the warm, vibrant speaking voice of the author, the book's variety—in content, shape, and style—is also fascinating. It is a miscellany, or to use Traill's analogy, a collection of "pearls and pebbles:"

    ...if you glean but one bright glad thought from the pages of my little volume,
    or add but one pearl to your store of knowledge from the experience of the

now-aged naturalist, she will not think the time has been wasted that has been spent in gathering the pebbles from notebooks and journals written during the long years of her life in the backwoods of Canada.

The book consists of a series of prose sketches, and some poetry. The chief focus is Canadian natural history: native flora and fauna as Traill observes them in the 1890s; as they were in the 1830s when she came to Canada; and as they may become in the next century. But her topic is not limited to the environment, and several chapters describe pioneer life in Upper Canada. Moreover, within chapters, topics frequently overlap, so that a single sketch becomes a tapestry of interwoven textual strands. Stylistically too, miscellany rules as Traill mingles meditation, anecdote, reminiscence, and detached scientific observation. Although Traill's voice controls the work, other voices are heard, both in the frequent citations of poetry and prose and in the inclusion of other speakers, as in the female narrator of "Alone in the Forest." The result is a multi-faceted, never-dull volume with a broad appeal, certain to be as popular now as it was over a century ago.

One of the many facets of *Pearls and Pebbles* is its autobiographical quality; it provides details of Traill's life—and encompasses ninety years of that life! The book opens with "Pleasant Days of My Childhood," a reflective, nostalgic reminiscence of the Strickland family's celebration of May Day, long ago in England. "Pleasant Days" sets forth the author's love for her family, a bond that was maintained by letters, even when Catharine had emigrated to Canada. And in Canada, the other two Strickland emigrants, Susanna Moodie and Samuel Strickland, were always in close contact with their sister Catharine. In addition, the first chapter establishes Catharine's position as a family favourite, "an especial pet in the household." As the biographical introduction to the first edition makes clear,[2] Catharine, the cheerful loving child, kept the qualities that endeared her to others into adulthood and old age. In her interesting and anecdotal biography of Catharine Traill, Mary Agnes FitzGibbon involves a few of her great-aunt's many admirers including in the number, such pre-eminent figures as Sandford Fleming, later to be knighted for his achievements and become Sir Sandford Fleming. Traill might have lacked money, but she certainly never lacked friends!

The second sketch, "Sunset and Sunrise on Lake Ontario," overtly autobiographical, is taken from Traill's diary of 1832 and describes the Traills' arrival in Brockville, Upper Canada, and their progress through the Thousand Islands on their way to settlement in the backwoods. As autobiography, it completes and fleshes out Letter 4 of Traill's account of pioneering, *The Backwoods of Canada*. In "Sunset and Sunrise" we meet a confident young woman who is ready to face her new life. It is interesting to note that, even with hindsight and with the personal experience of hardship and disaster in the backwoods, Traill does not edit out the optimism, hinting only at future difficulties. She remembers herself, "Charmed by the romantic natural beauties of the surrounding scene, [so that] no dread of the future rose up to oppress me."

The autobiographical quality of *Pearls and Pebbles* is further enhanced by Mary Agnes FitzGibbon's introduction to the first text.[3] Mary Agnes was Traill's grandniece, daughter of Agnes FitzGibbon Chamberlin, who collaborated with Traill on *Canadian Wild Flowers* (1868), and granddaughter of Susanna Moodie. Mary Agnes was a well-known writer herself.[4] This, plus the family circumstances ideally position Mary Agnes to discuss knowledgeably Traill's life and work. Because she includes long passages from her great-aunt's journals, Traill's voice is heard, so that the third person narration of biography becomes the first person narration of autobiography. What results, then, is a picture of Traill's life story as she perceives it and wishes it to be told.

All other sketches are autobiographical to some extent, taken from Traill's journals[5] and might well be discussed solely in that light. Through a reading of *Pearls and Pebbles* we meet a happy, practical and devout woman (who frequently cites from or paraphrases the Bible, prayer book or hymnal), a woman who is infinitely curious about the world around her—even in her nineties, she continues to wonder and to speculate. When she digs up a strange "glittering" lizard in the 1890s, for example, she says, "I transferred it to my flower pot and carried it home that I might study it more at my leisure." The narrator of *Pearls and Pebbles* is warmly inquisitive and often intrusive. It is impossible to avoid her; it is equally impossible to dislike her.

But *Pearls and Pebbles* is more than autobiography. It shows an earlier time in Canadian history, and thus becomes an important historical document. While historical details creep into most sketches, three speak specifically of pioneer life: "Sunset and Sunrise on Lake Ontario," "The First Death in the Clearing" and "Alone in the Forest."

When the Traills emigrated in 1832, much of Ontario was only sparsely settled. Backbreaking and often heartbreaking labour accompanied efforts to conquer the centuries-old Canadian forest. The task proved especially formidable for British middle-class emigrants like the Traills, who were unaccustomed to manual labour. Catharine Traill has documented some of her experiences in *The Backwoods of Canada* and *The Canadian Settler's Guide* and in numerous periodical pieces.[6]

"Sunset and Sunrise" is an appropriate place to begin a discussion of pioneering in Canada, for it features the pioneer's arrival. The piece captures a typical spirit of heady optimism, a mood enhanced by small-town celebrations—a boat launching, a wedding. Even nature conspires, providing a "glorious" sunset for the emigrant. In the chapter, Traill provides a brief portrait of a Canadian town of the 1830s and describes the landscape of the Thousand Islands; both are seen through a rosy lens and are interpreted with the hope and confidence of the untested new arrival. Traill only hints at what is to come.

"The First Death," anecdotal in style, occurs at a later date (appearing, appropriately, later in the text), and more definitely establishes the daunting task of pioneering. It centres on one of Traill's backwoods neighbours, a woman with a dying baby. Certain harsh facts emerge: the nonstop drudgery of a pioneer woman's life (Traill must return home to attend to her family and Jessie must feed the mill hands), not to mention the high death rate of children at the time. Yet the women show courage as they support each other; even the little messenger girl is part of a supportive female network, extending a hand to Traill to help her through the swamp. This community of women cannot prevent death, but they can work together and, as Mary Agnes FitzGibbon says in her biography of her great-aunt, Jessie never forgot her neighbor's sympathetic assistance:

> Last summer when Mrs. Traill was so ill that few thought she would recover, Jessie's grief was great. She recalled over and over again the kindness to her in the bush in those early days.

A portrait of pioneer life emerges in these pages; this is a harsh world made bearable only through hard work and co-operation.

As is typical of Traill's writing, however, other elements are at play in the sketch, helping to create a miscellany. For one thing, the anecdote becomes personal when Traill reveals that she too has lost infant children (Mary Ellen and Eleanor): "I did my best to comfort her, although I had not then known the pang of a bereaved mother's heart. God gave me that trial in after years." For another thing, the narrative borders on allegory: the child's death occurs in spring, which when coupled with Traill's dusk-to-dawn watch over the baby, has ties with Easter and Christian symbolism. In this fashion, an historical sketch takes on added significance, becoming at once personal / autobiographical and religious / allegorical.

A similar compounding of miscellany appears in the anecdote "Alone in the Forest." As demonstrated here, Canada could be a hostile place, physically, socially and financially. The sketch ostensibly deals with the plight of a woman lost at night in the bush and the unmarked or poorly marked bush trails, not to mention sparse settlement, made this a real and present danger to the pioneer. "Alone in the Forest" sets forth a few less obvious perils of pioneering, too. First, as an emigrant British gentlewoman, Traill's narrator finds the backwoods socially threatening, actually being frightened by the hospitable Irish family who give her shelter:

> I was startled by the sight of mine host, whose keen, black eyes were bent on me with, as I thought, a sinister, inquisitive look, such that I shrunk affrighted from before him.

Second, poverty could dash the emigrant's hope for a better future: "for truly misfortune like an armed force came soon upon them, and every fair and flattering prospect vanished." Canada might well defeat the emigrant faced with these woes—she could be lost, figuratively and literally, unable to cope. Or the pioneer might learn new ways and survive—she could find her way to safety and use privation to develop "a courage and strength of mind to do and to bear."

The sketch is covertly autobiographical, for Traill's experiences mirror her narrator's. The Traills did not do well financially in Canada, and

Catharine Traill, as an English gentlewoman, must have suffered at least some sense of social dislocation in the rough and ready bush society. Still, her buoyant spirit, bolstered by a strong religious faith, seems to have sustained her throughout strikingly similar circumstances.

A third key attribute of *Pearls and Pebbles*, and arguably the most important, is the author's interest in natural history. Except for the opening chapter, all sketches deal with the Canadian landscape, and through Traill, we are introduced to such diverse organisms as mosses, trees, birds, flowers, spiders and salamanders.

At points, Traill's observations are specific, accurate, couched in the scientific jargon of the era and employing latinate terms. A self-taught amateur, Traill has a keen eye for detail, labelling and naming what she sees and, in the process, leaving a record of Canadian life forms, some of which have disappeared or are hard to find today. In her scientific reporting, Traill does not rely entirely on her own knowledge; rather, she cites expert sources to verify her work. Thomas McIlwraith's *Birds of Ontario* (1884) is a favorite reference. And various friends voice their opinions as, for example, do Mr. Stewart in "More About My Feathered Friends" and Mr. E____ in "Prospecting." Traill's knowledge seems extensive enough for her purposes; nevertheless, she strengthens her comments and adds to the miscellany through deferential quotations.

As she observes the landscape, listing, naming, defining and so on, Traill ponders the significance of what she sees—and does not see. Since the book was written over a sixty-year period, she can remark on the metamorphosis of the landscape, noting changes in flora and fauna that appear to have been an inevitable result of pioneering. In this sense, Traill has an ecological awareness that is far ahead of her time. Because she has been a pioneer, Traill argues for change, but as a naturalist, she laments the passing of the old ways and the loss of indigenous life forms. Ultimately, Traill's analysis of connections between man and his environment has significance today, as we too face the continued destruction of the natural world in the name of "progress."

In "Memories of a May Morning," dated 1888, Traill notices the delayed arrival of snow sparrows, crossbills and tom-tits in spring, and blames the absence on environmental change:

In mild winters they were wont to come as early as the middle of March, but
that was in the early days of the colony, when the thick forests gave warm
shelter to the wild birds; but since the trees are fast disappearing the snow
sparrows and crossbills (Loxia curvirostra), and the tom-tits or black caps, and
many others, delay their coming till April or even May.

Traill pursues this line of inquiry in "More About My Feathered Friends,"
saying that the Scarlet Tanager is "now rare" because it "loves the seclusion of the quiet woods, far from the noisy haunts of men." She goes on to
implicate pioneers in the tanager's disappearance:

> During my first year's residence in the Douro backwoods, I used to watch eager-
> ly for the appearance of these beautiful scarlet birds... As the woods are cleared
> away we lose many of our summer visitors from the other side of the lakes.

Sadly, neither at the time of her writing nor today is there any indication
that the gradual process of loss has ended.

"Notes from My Old Diary" allows for similar speculation, as in the 1890s
Traill looks at notes written in the 1830s. With hindsight she can say:

> There is a change in the country; many of the plants and birds and wild crea-
> tures, common once, have disappeared entirely before the march of civiliza-
> tion. As the woods which shelter them are cleared away, they retire to the lone-
> ly forest haunts still left, where they may remain unmolested and unseen till
> again driven back by the advance of man upon the scene.

The trees which "shelter" the bush's inhabitants are seen by the settler
as obstacles to success; accordingly, in the process of pioneering, trees
are ruthlessly cut down and native life forms vanish. Although herself a
pioneer, and thereby implicated in the destruction, Traill portrays the pioneer's arrival in warlike terms: as man "advances" in his "march of civilization" plants, birds and "wild creatures" retreat or are "driven back."
The telling diction reveals Traill's ecological bias.

A later chapter, "In the Canadian Woods," celebrates the Canadian bush
—which had almost disappeared in southern Ontario by 1894. Like "Notes
from My Old Diary," it adds an 1890s perspective to earlier journal entries

and the sketch serves, in part, as Traill's elegiac memorial to a landscape she had loved, even while she helped to destroy it. The forest here is animated, full of active life, and Traill describes a myriad of life forms, all sorts of trees, flowers, birds, animals. Even the earth is alive—female and fecund:

> The earth is teeming with luxuriance, and one might almost fancy her conscious of all the wealth of vegetable treasures she bears on her capacious breast, and which she has brought forth and nourished.

Readers become actively involved in the animated world; we are invited to join the narrator on a walk through the bush: "Here is a pathway under the maples and beeches; let us follow it." Once inside, we discover a great deal of activity: sap flows up the trees; animals and birds move in and among the trees; leaves flutter in the wind; a "kindly little evergreen" is discovered "[c]reeping over little hillocks in shady ground." The spectator's senses are bombarded by the colours, smells, and sounds of a beautiful, but perpetually busy place. Added to the constant spatial movement is a temporal movement created by Traill's use of the cycle of the seasons to shape the narrative. By beginning with the bush in spring and ending in winter, Traill places her observations within an eternal, cyclic pattern.

Yet many references remind us that the ongoing cycle has been broken by the pioneers. One season is no longer like all preceding seasons. As Traill remarks, "the ruthless advance of man upon the scene, in cutting down the sheltering trees," has not only caused the late arrival of spring flowers, but "[s]ome indeed of the forest plants have disappeared and we see them no more." Similarly, Indian Summer has ceased to be a predictable phenomenon:

> There is a change in the climate since the time when we used to look for the Indian Summer. The destruction of the forest trees has told upon it in many ways. We feel it in the sweep of the wind in autumn and spring especially, in the drifting snow of winter, and in the growing scarcity of the fish in our lakes.

Such comments sound an alarm. Words like "growing scarcity" and "destruction," coupled with Traill's obvious love of the bush as it was, move her writing beyond factual reporting into ecological elegy.

"In the Canadian Woods" concludes with a section on winter, where, rather belatedly, there is an obvious and somewhat awkward shift in point of view, as Traill modifies her position and her pioneer voice reasserts itself. From this stance, change is good and necessary, and Traill reiterates the increased good fortune of the emigrant. As elsewhere, she provides a comprehensive list of items that have vanished:

> ...the log house, the primeval settlement house; the disfiguring stump in the newly-cleared fallows; the ugly snake-like rail fence, the rude enclosures of the first efforts of the immigrant.

Although she repeats a by-now-familiar writing formula, listing and documenting appearances and disappearances, she now works to a different end. The ugly, undesirable objects listed above, denoting the emigrant's initial poverty and struggle to survive, have been replaced by beautiful objects, denoting wealth and comfort:

> Fair dwellings, tasteful gardens, fruitful orchards, the village schoolhouse, the church spire, the busy factory, the iron-girdered bridge, the steamboat, the railroad, the telegraph, the telephone.

Traill juxtaposes her lists and her landscapes to argue that change is necessary. Through pioneering, a greater good is achieved and a picturesque, prosperous and peopled landscape is the new ideal.

Almost immediately Traill undercuts her justification of the removal of the forest, as the poem, "A Song for a Sleigh Drive," which closes out the chapter, reverts to elegy and loss. Even though she praises progress in the final stanza when she says, "For the bright golden grain / Shall wave o'er the plain," the force of the sentiment is diminished by the stanza's opening and closing laments: "Oh, wail for the forest! The green shady forest!"; and "Oh, wail for the forest, its glories are o'er."

"Something Gathers Up the Fragments" ends the book and represents Traill's final attempt to resolve the naturalist – pioneer duality. Traill looks at the interdependence of nature, the eternal cyclic patterns of growth and decay, following the life cycle of a tree—how it had been "sustained" by the earth while it was alive:

Never idle were those vegetable miners, always digging materials from the
dark earth to add power and substance to the tree, hour by hour building up
its wonderful structure, taking and selecting only such particles as were suited to increase the woody fibre and add to the particular qualities of the tree,
whether it be oak, or ash, or maple, or the majestic pine.

Nor has the tree merely taken from its surroundings; like all living organisms in the forest, the tree also has given something back: "fresh matter,
in the form of leaves, decayed branches and effete bark and fruitful seed."
Now that it has fallen, and as it decomposes, it provides a home for lichens
and mosses. Finally, it will become a "rich black vegetable mould." The
process of growth and decomposition is cyclic, an ongoing process that
endured for countless numbers of years—until the arrival of the pioneers:

Then comes man, a settler in the forest wilderness, a stranger and an emigrant
from a far-off land. Coming to make himself a home, he must cut down the living trees and clear the ground with axe and fire.

Although the diction (fire, struggle, death) still attests to a troubled con-
science, and while the reference to human involvement in the forest is
limited to only a few sentences (the forest takes over the sketch), Traill
concludes that God is directing change: "Disorder—order unperceived by
thee; / All chance—direction which thou canst not see." Further, she
resolves that the cycle of nature has been designed solely to prepare the
soil "to receive the grain for the life-sustaining bread" of the emigrant and
his family. And she reinforces her position with two Biblical citations:
"Something gathers up the fragments, and nothing is lost;" and "Whoso
is wise, and will observe these things, even they shall understand the loving kindness of the Lord." Catharine Traill may have satisfied herself with
this explanation, but a contemporary reader is more likely to be swayed
by her ecological distrust of change than by her Christian resolution.

Perhaps no book is more suitable for republication at the end of the twentieth century than Catharine Parr Traill's *Pearls and Pebbles*. Through a mix-
ture of pioneer tales, personal anecdotes and reminiscences, botanical and
zoological observations, astute ecological comments, not to mention poetry,
this talented, intelligent woman, with an apparently boundless energy and

love of life, creates a collage of nineteenth-century Canadian life. The work is by turns anecdotal, reflective, scientific and discursive. Each genre is interesting in its own right, and there is something for everyone in these pages—the historian, the scientist, the ecologist, the poet, or, simply, the lover of life. Of great significance to a contemporary reader is Traill's understanding of the connection between man and his environment, for Traill has an ecological awareness that is far ahead of her time. Even as she celebrates the accomplishments of the pioneers, she laments the irretrievable loss of plants, animals and people, for in her eyes, the Native Canadians may also disappear with the removal of the forest. As a pioneer settler herself, she is aware of her complicity in the destruction of an ecosystem, and her work resonates with an unresolved tension. Has she improved or destroyed the landscape? Compare this with our own ecological concerns, as, at the end of a century, we enumerate losses and gains. Have we indeed come so very far? Our concerns are distressingly similar to those voiced by a very old woman in 1894.

EDITING PROCEDURE

So that the reader may "see" the book as it originally appeared, little has been changed from the original text. For one thing, Traill's explanatory footnotes have been kept as in the original. For another, when Traill cites other writers, whether poetry or prose, their words are set off from the text by means of quotation marks; this practice has been maintained. Traill's own poetry is not set off with quotation marks, but is incorporated into the text. Again the original model has been followed here. While this was standard nineteenth-century procedure, today's readers may need to be alerted to the practice.

Some changes have been made. The original introduction by Mary Agnes FitzGibbon now appears as Appendix A. FitzGibbon's work is an important part of the text, for it features several of Traill's unpublished "pearls"—anecdotes, descriptions, and observations that she had considered publishing. In addition, it provides a splendid overview of Traill's life, biased perhaps, because it is written by someone who obviously loves her great-aunt dearly, but essential reading none the less. Where possible, endnotes identify Traill's citations of poetry, prose, and scripture. At the time of publication, most references would have been familiar to her readers which explains her lack of consistent notation. Times and tastes change, though, and many passages are now obscure, making endnoting useful. Even the editor failed to find a few references despite searching all the obvious, and a few not so obvious places. One poem turned up in an Elementary School Reader! The editor would like to hear from readers who can identify the remaining quotations. Endnotes also identify work that was previously published by Traill. It should also be mentioned that Traill rewrote material constantly, and, as a result, fragments from most sketches in *Pearls and Pebbles* appear throughout her writing—some in published material, others in the journals and letters. Because of her tendency to recycle her ideas, a complete listing of previous references is impossible in this edition. As for the Biblical references, the approach has been to identify the direct citation. The indirect references which are incorporated into the text are too numerous to mention. Traill's frequent use of scripture is a trademark of her writing and reveals the woman's deeply sincere religiosity. The 1894 edition included illustrations, four of which appear here: a portrait of Catharine Parr Traill ("Yours Very Truly"), a sample of her handwriting, Reydon Hall, and Polly Cow's Island. This edition features additional visual material, as for example, two of the watercolour prints from *Canadian Wild Flowers*.

PEARLS
& PEBBLES

PREFACE

ALTHOUGH I lived the first few years of my childhood at Stowe House, near Bungay, in the lovely valley of the Waveney, most of my young life was spent at Reydon Hall, an old Elizabethan mansion in the eastern part of the county of Suffolk, and within easy walk of the sea-coast town of Southwold, now a much more frequented resort than in former days.

Business or pleasure often led us to the town, and the beach was a great attraction and source of pleasure to my sisters and myself. We loved to watch the advance and recoil of the waves, the busy fishermen among their nets and boats, and the groups of happy children on the sands; but there was a greater fascination still to us in the search for treasures left by the flood tide or cast upon the shore by the ever restless waves.

Sometimes there was little to reward the seekers, but hope was ever before us, and the finding of shining stones—red, yellow and white—bits of jet or amber, a shell or lovely seaweed, to be deposited in bag or basket, would send us home jubilant to add to the hoarded store of fossils and other garnered treasures, or to show to the dear mother, who would turn the treasures over and say with a smile, "Let me see what precious pearls my Katie has found among her many pebbles hardly worth bringing home."

Still the time was not wholly wasted. Health and pleasure had been gained with my pebbles, and had there been but one pearl among them, the simple heart of the little maiden had been well content.

So, my readers, if you glean but one bright glad thought from the pages of my little volume, or add but one pearl to your store of knowledge from the experience of the now aged naturalist, she will not think the time wasted that has been spent in gathering the pebbles from notebooks and journals written during the long years of her life in the backwoods of Canada.

"WESTOVE," LAKEFIELD,
    September 20, 1894.

PLEASANT DAYS OF MY CHILDHOOD

"How dear to this heart are the scenes of my childhood,
When fond recollection presents them to view!
The orchard, the meadow, the deep-tangled wildwood,
And every loved spot which my infancy knew."[1]

THERE is something almost magical in the word May. It brings back to memory pictures of all things sweet and fair that charmed us in our youthful days; it recalls the joys of infancy when we filled our laps with flowers.

We hear again the song of blackbird, linnet and robin, and the far-away call of that mystery of childhood, the cuckoo. We hear the murmur of the summer wind among the rustling green flags beside the river; we scent the flowers of the hawthorn, and the violets hidden among the grass, and fill our hands with bluebells and cowslips.

But we have in Canada few such May days as Shakespeare, Milton and Herrick describe; here too often it may be said that "Winter, lingering, chills the lap of May."[2]

The inborn sense of the beautiful springs to life in the soul of the babe when it stretches forth an eager hand to grasp the flowers in its nurse's bosom. It is the birth of a new and pleasurable emotion. I love to see an innocent child playing with the fresh fair flowers, meet emblems at once of its own beauty and frailty; for does not the Word say, "He cometh forth like a flower, and is cut down."[3]

It was on the banks of that most beautiful of Suffolk rivers, the Waveney, that the first happy years of my childhood were passed. My father's family came from the north of England, where among the mountain dales and fells still lingered many primitive customs and ancient rural sports. Of these the keeping of May Day—no doubt a relic of some ancient pagan rite, but, the origin forgotten, now perfectly harmless—was one of the most cherished. My father still clung to the old observance of this rural holiday of his ancestors, and May Day was looked forward to with eager anticipation by my sisters and myself.

The flowers—the sweet May blossoms of the hawthorn hedge and the early spring flowers—must be gathered while the dew was still upon them, or the rites lost half their virtue.

We were always up before the sun, and so eagerly did we watch for the day that even our dreams were haunted by the anticipated pleasure, for I remember my mother telling of being startled in the night by seeing the door softly open and a small white-robed figure glide up to the bedside. It was Sara, her eyes wide open, fixed and staring, but the child was fast asleep. Two tiny hands held up the full folds of her nightdress as she said, "Flowers, more flowers, Lila." Even in her sleep she had gathered dream-flowers for the May Day garlands.

I was the youngest but one, and being an especial pet in the household, on my happy head was conferred the May crown, and I was duly greeted as Queen of May.

Surely no queen could have been more joyous or proud of her honors: my crown, a circlet of flowers, my sceptre a flower-wreathed wand of hazel, and my throne a mound of daisy-sprinkled turf in the meadow by the clear flowing river; my loyal subjects, the dearest and most loving of sisters.

The crown so coveted was worn till night, and then cast aside to wither in the dust. *Sic transit gloria mundi!*[4]

Within a short distance of the old house there was a narrow bridlepath which we called the "little lane," It was shut in from the main road, with which it ran parallel, by a quick-set hedge; on the other side were high sloping banks, the unfenced boundary of upland pastures.

On the grassy slopes grew tall oak trees and a tangled jungle of wild bushes, among which woodbine and sweet briar entwined, forming luxuriant bowers, beneath which all sorts of flowers grew in rich profusion.

On the other, or lower side of the land, a little tinkling rill, that a child might step across, ran down, its water clear and bright. From this slender streamlet we children drank the most draughts from Nature's own chalice, the hollow of our hands, or sipped its pure waters, like the fairies we read of, from the acorn cups that strewed the grass.

The banks of the stream were lined with sweet purple violets, primroses, and the little sun-bright celandine; and later on there was good store of wild strawberries, which we gathered and strung upon a stalk of grass to carry home to our mother as a peace-offering for torn frocks and soiled pinafores, or leave out-stayed.

This charming spot was our Eden. In it we laid out beds and planted a garden for ourselves. Like Canadian squatters, we took to ourselves right of soil, and made a free settlement *sans ceremonie*. The garden was laid out right daintily. The beds were planted with double daisies and many garden bulbs and flowers discarded or begged from the gardener's parterres. A hollow in the bank was fashioned into a grotto, which we lined with moss and decorated with dry striped snailshells and bright stones.

Our garden tools were of the rudest—our trowel a rusty iron ladle, our spade a broken-bladed carving knife, and we daily watered the flowers from a battered tin teapot and a leaky japanned mug. But in spite of these unhandy implements, the garden throve and blossomed in the wilderness.

There, sheltered from sun and shower among the bowery honeysuckles, we reclined on the green turf, happy as children could be, and listened to the oft-repeated stories and old ballads that were recited by our two elder sisters. How we delighted in those tales and quaint old rhymes, and how little we dreamed that the time would come when the sisters who regaled us with them would make a name for themselves in the world of letters.*

Many years afterwards I visited the "little lane." A few crocuses and snowdrops, choked by long grass and weeds, were all that were left to mark the spot where "once a garden smiled."[5]

I stooped and as of old drank of the bright little stream, and gathered a nosegay of the sweet violets to carry away as a *souvenir* of my childhood. Often in after years have the memories of those May days among the

*Elizabeth and Agnes Strickland.

cowslips and daisied meads of the Waveney come back to my wearied soul to cheer and soothe the exile in her far distant forest home.

LAMENT FOR THE MAY QUEEN

Weep, weep, thou virgin Queen of May,
    Thy ancient reign is o'er;
Thy vot'ries now are lowly laid,
    And thou art Queen no more.

Fling down, fling down, thy flow'ry crown,
    Thy sceptre cast away,
For ne'er again on vale or plain
    They'll hail thee Queen of May.

No maiden now with glowing brow
    Shall rise with early dawn,
To bind her hair with chaplets fair
    Torn from the blossomed thorn.

No lark shall spring on dewy wing
    Thy matin hymn to pour,
No cuckoo's voice shall shout, "Rejoice!"
    For thou art Queen no more.

Beneath thy flower-encircled wand
    No peasant trains advance;
No more they lead with sportive tread
    The merry, merry dance.

The violet blooms with modest grace
    Beneath its crest of leaves;
The primrose shows her gentle face,
    Her wreaths the woodbine weaves.

The cowslip bends her golden head,
    And daisies deck the lea;
But ah! no more in grove or bower
    The Queen of May we'll see.[6]

SUNSET AND SUNRISE ON LAKE ONTARIO:
A REMINISCENCE*

"To watch the dimmed day deepen into even,
   The flush of sunset melt in pallid gold;
While the pale planets blossom out in heaven;
   To feel the tender silence trance and hold
The night's great heartbeats; soul-washed, nature-shriven,
   To feel the mantle of silence fold on fold."
                              —*William Wilfr[e]d Campbell*[1]

OUR steamer had been lying all day in front of the town of Brockville. It was a gala day in that place. There had been a successful launch of a new-ly-built schooner to excite the townsfolk and attract strangers from the American side across the St. Lawrence.

A military band was playing, and flags flew from the steeples of the churches—on every public building, indeed, was seen the Union Jack in friendly unison with the Stars and Stripes.

The bells of the town rang cheerily in honor of a wedding party, who later came on board our vessel on their honeymoon trip to Niagara. Our departure was delayed by the taking in of freight for the upper provincial towns, and the landing of such as had been forwarded to Brockville, as

---

*A page from my old diary, August, 1832.

well as by the late arrival of a number of extra passengers, so that it was well on towards evening before we left the wharf and entered the intricate channels of the Lake of the Thousand Isles.

The day had been excessively hot, and grateful was the change to the cool refreshing shades of the wooded islands, where oak and ash and elm mingled their branches with those of the dark feathery hemlock, pine and balsam firs. The grey cedars, too, delighted the eye which had become wearied with the glare of the sun upon the glassy surface of the water.

Our progress was slow and steady, for in those early days of steam navigation much caution was shown, and truly the passenger immigrants on board were in no hurry, for the "wide world was all before them, where to choose their place of rest."[2]

Every turn of the paddlewheels brought some new and lovely spot into view. Visions of pleasant rustic homes to be made by forest, lake and river rose to my mental vision as our vessel threaded her way among those fairy islands; and with almost childish delight I would point out wild rocky headlands bright with golden lichens and deep green velvet mosses, or inland coves half hidden by drooping ferns and native willows or red with the changeful crimson of the glossy-leafed American Creeper (*Ampelopsis Virginica*), which was already wreathing in gorgeous autumnal colors the silvery bark of the graceful birches and elms.

What tufts of goldenrod and pale bluebells, what starry asters were mirrored in the calm waters! What glorious spikes of cardinal lobelias and azure-fringed gentians were growing wild and free on many a rugged spot where possibly no foot of man had ever trodden!

The captain said it would be midnight ere we reached Kingston, the "Limestone City," and dawn before we could be at Cobourg, where our voyage was to terminate. Thence our way would lie northward to what was at that time the *ultima thule*[3] of civilization a forest wilderness beyond the infant settlement of the new village of Peterborough,* then but a cluster of log houses and squatters' shanties.

Charmed by the romantic natural beauties of the surrounding scene, no dread of the future rose up to oppress me. Truly distance lent its enchantment to cheer and animate my spirits.[4]

---

*Now a city of no mean importance in Ontario.

Brockville, St. Lawrence, by W.H Bartlett, in Willis' *Canadian Scenery* (1848).

The sun set that evening in a flood of rose and amber, coloring the waveless surface of the lake with a radiance such as my English eyes had never yet looked upon.

How lovely it was! My husband smiled at my enthusiasm. Had he ever beheld so glorious a sunset before?

"Yes, many a time, in Italy and in Switzerland: often quite as beautiful."

I wished to claim all the loveliness for Canada, the country of our adoption and henceforth our home.

The afterglow of rose tints faded only to give place to the tremulous rays of the now risen moon, giving a yet greater charm to the scenery, deepening the shadows or throwing objects into stronger relief. Then, later on, as star after star came out, heaven seemed to cast unnumbered glories at our feet in these twinkling points of light mirrored in the lake. Almost unconsciously the inspired words rose to my lips, "The heavens declare the glory of God, and the firmament showeth His handiwork."[5]

Wrapped in my ample Scotch tartan cloak, I lay with head pillowed on my husband's folded plaid, too much delighted with my surroundings to leave the deck for the cabin and the sleeping berth below.

Scene Among the Thousand Isles, by W.H. Bartlett, in Willis' *Canadian Scenery* (1848).

Sometimes our vessel passed so near the rocks that the overhanging boughs of the trees almost swept the sides of the smokestack, startling from their night roosts flocks of blackbirds and pigeons. Flying out they circled around us, then settled again among the trees. The distant hooting of the big cat-owl was the only sound that broke the monotonous plash of the paddlewheels. The only other living thing that I noted was the motionless figure of a heron standing on a fallen cedar overhanging the margin of the water. When our approach disturbed her night watch for prey, she spread her grey wings and noiselessly flew onward to take her stand once more on some other prostrate tree. There was a sort of witch-like weirdness about this lonely watcher of the waters,[6] such that I could not help but follow her silent, mysterious flight and observe the shadow of her wings upon the lake.

Fascinated by the bird, I watched her until weariness overtook my senses, when my eyes closed and I slept so soundly that it was not till the clanging bell gave notice to the passengers that we were nearing the site of the frontier town of Cobourg that I awoke.

If the night had been lovely, so also was the dawn, as the sun rose in robes of the most exquisite colors. The boat was now bearing in nearer to the shores of what appeared to be a rolling country, all clothed with forest green.

Hill rising above hill came out from the clouds of morning mist, far away to the distant northern limits of the horizon, till mingling with the grey they melted into a mere cloud line to the eye.

Around us, gilded by the rays of the rising sun, the smooth surface of the lake shone like a sea of gold, the spray from the paddlewheels catching a thousand rainbow hues as it fell. Surpassingly beautiful were the clouds of mist as they broke into all sorts of fanciful forms, rising higher and higher, anon taking the appearance of islands, above which the dark fringe of forest-clothed shores was visible, while the white creamy vapors below made mimic lakes and streams.

Then in a moment all was changed. The mirage of the shadowy landscape disappeared; a breath of cool air from the water separated the mist and lifted it like a gold-tinted veil, high above the trees, capes, islands, bays and forest-crowned headlands, until all faded away, leaving but a dream of beauty on the gazer's mind—a memory to be recalled in after years when musing over past scenes of a life where lights and shadows form a mingled pattern of trials and blessings.

MEMORIES OF A MAY MORNING*

꒛

> "Sweet day, so cool, so calm, so bright,
> The bridal of the earth and sky;
> The dew shall weep thy fall to-night,
> For thou must die."
>
> —*Herbert*[1]

JUST such a day as holy as George Herbert describes above is this sweet May morning. But what a change since yesterday in the temperature of the air! Then chilling northeast winds, grey cloudy sky, cold and cheerless; now, bright cloudless blue sky and soft balmy airs.

Yesterday I was wrapped in a thick woollen shawl over my shoulders, and a warm quilted hood on my head. Today my morning wrapper of printed calico and my muslin cap are all-sufficient for warmth; hood and shawl are laid aside.

Our spring is unusually late this year; the leaves are not unfolded. I lie upon the couch on the veranda basking in the delicious warmth of the sun's rays as they reach me through the half-clothed branches of the maple and beech trees in the grove beyond my garden. I recall last year at this same date when all the trees were in leaf and the plum and apple trees in full bloom. We are three weeks later this year. Well, it is folly to complain

---

*From my diary of 1888.

of the vicissitudes of the seasons; let us take the blessings as they come to us and be thankful—the leaves and buds and blossoms are all before us. It is a pleasure to lie here and watch the birds as they flit to and fro so gaily among the trees and garden shrubs, carolling and twittering in the unalloyed gladness of their nature quite heedless of my presence. Let me see who of my old acquaintances are among them. There are the neat little snow sparrows (*Junco hyemalis*), which are among the first and most constant of the small birds to visit us, coming from the cold Northwest to make spring and summer holiday in our more genial climate. In mild winters they were wont to come as early as the middle of March, but that was in the early days of the colony, when the thick forests gave warm shelter to the wild

"Westove, Lakefield."

birds; but since the trees are fast disappearing the snow sparrows and crossbills (*Loxia curvirostra*), and the tom-tits or black-caps,* and many others, delay their coming till April or even May. I used to call the pretty snow sparrows my "quaker birds," when first I saw them and did not know their name. I admired their exquisitely neat plumage of slate-grey, white breast, darker head, flesh-colored bills and legs and feet, with some snow-white feathers at the tail, and the edges of the long shaft feathers of their wings also tipped with white. They looked so tidy and delicate, as if no speck or spot could sully their quakerly neat dress.

These birds usually appear in company with the small brown and the chestnut-crowned sparrows,† with which they seem to be on the most friendly terms, mixing with them as they flit about the garden seeking for seeds among the dry amaranths and other weeds.

*Chickadee of the Americans—*Parus atricapillus*.
†Chipping sparrow—*Spizella socialis*.

The snowbirds and their friends, the chipping sparrows, are busy now in the bushes in the grove building their nests. In this they have no time to lose, as the season is so late.

A lively burst of song greets me just above my head, in the angle of the beams of the veranda. How well I know those cheerful notes. It is the dear little brown house wren's song.

Yes, there they are, the bright little couple. They look down shyly at me from their coign of vantage above; and then, as if quite sure it is an old and trusted friend they burst out with a joyous chorus of greeting as if to say:

"Here we are again; glad to see you alive and well, old lady." And the old lady looks up, and nods a hearty welcome to the tiny brown birds.

It is now more than twenty years since a pair of these little wrens came and took possession of that corner of the veranda, just where the angle of the rafters meet the roof—a dark, snug little place. There, year after year, every May, a pair return to the old spot.

It can hardly be the same old couple, or even their children or grandchildren, that are such constant visitors, never at a loss, but coming at once to the old corner, where, after a few days' rest, they commence to build a rudely-constructed nest of birch twigs; no moss, nor hair, nor any soft materials are employed for the cradles of the tiny little brood.

What brings these tiny birds back to the old summer haunts? is it memory? Or is it that unerring, mysterious power that we term INSTINCT, which, acting like an irresistible impulse, guides them the right way, straight to the harbor where they would be?

Is it this that draws the fledglings of last year back to the nest in which they were reared, to re-enact the life and habits of the parent birds of the particular species of the wren family to which they especially belong? We know not.

For the first week after they arrive the wrens do nothing but flit gaily about, making high holiday with merry songs before they settle down to work in good earnest.

The first thing they do is to clear away the old rubbish from last year's nest—a regular course of housecleaning—before the foundation of the new nest is laid. In the work of building both labor. They are not selfish, my dear little household pets, like some of the male birds, which leave all the work of building and care of the nurslings to the female, while they take their ease, eating and singing and enjoying themselves.

The wrens arrive just before the first hatch of the Mayflies issue from their watery prison. It is with the smaller ephemera, the two-oared flies, that they feed their young.

Is it not marvellous the instinct which impels these little birds to return at the exact time of the year to where the particular kind of nourishment required for the little broods can only be obtained?

O wondrous law, given by their Creator to each one of His creatures, in accordance with His will and their several needs!

All day long, from sunrise to sunset, these birds are on the wing, as soon as the little ones are hatched, going and coming unweariedly, with a love for their offspring that never tires.

Listen to the song of greeting they give to the nestling as they drop the fly into the open beak, having first torn off its stiff gauzy wings. This is a constant habit, and it is very dexterously done. In an instant the birds are again on the wing, to supply the ceaseless cravings of the greedy little ones, who seem ever to be crying out, "Give, give," when they hear the approach of the father or mother.

Last summer our wrens raised three successive broods. I do not think the number exceeded five little birds each time. This year the time will not admit of an extra hatch.

House Wren, by Thomas McIlwraith, in *Birds of Ontario* (1894).

The wrens usually linger with us till the end of August, but some will stay into September if the weather remains warm. Then they leave us to winter in a milder climate westward or southward, crossing the St. Lawrence or Niagara rivers guided by the same power that led them hither.

How little, after all, is our knowledge of the ways of these wild creatures that come to us, we only guess from whence.[2] They steal so quietly among us. One day they are seen building their temporary nests in our groves and forests, in our garden bushes and orchards, in the shade trees of our busiest streets, under the eaves of our houses and even of our churches and sacred temples; a few brief weeks or months, and lo! they disappear. Silently they came; as silently they depart.[3] Some, indeed, gather together in social bands, but others steal away unseen;[4] we know not how and when they go till we miss them, to see them no more again till the spring of another year.

While I am pondering over these mysteries, a pair of gay summer birds flash past me, evidently bent on important business. They are probably seeking a convenient bush where to commence the building of a nest for the reception of the unknown family.

I can fancy the lively discussion that is being carried on between the little pair, where to make choice of the best and safest situation for the nest.

That syringa opposite the drawing-room window is sure to be chosen. Every succeeding season it has had a nest built among its network of small branches, leaves and fragrant blossoms. It is the favorite resort of the little yellow birds.* Some call these birds "wild canaries," but there is a great difference between the species, the true wild canary being larger, of a pale lemon color, and the head marked in the male bird with a spot of black, also the wing feathers. It is a true finch, feeding on seeds, especially those of the thistle.

But I am interested in the movements of my little friends. There is evidently some demur about the fitness of the syringa bush—they seem to be debating between it and a Tartarian honeysuckle near the wicket gate—but time is pressing and a hasty choice must be made.

Yes, the faithful little pair have chosen the old syringa and are going to work at once.

Good-speed to you, my wise little couple. We shall soon see the result of your work, for I perceive your plans are all settled now.

Some two years ago a great event happened to a pair of my yellow birds, which ended in a serious disappointment. On warm May morning, as my daughter and I sat sewing on the veranda, a little passing puff of wind blew away some snips of the white material that we had been busy with and carried them among the grass just below the syringa bush, where the foundation of a nest had just been laid by the female bird. Her bright eyes quickly caught sight of the scraps of muslin, and down she came from her

---

*Yellow Warbler, or Summer Bird—*Dendroica œstiva.*

perch in the bush and carried off the prize to her nest, coming back and diligently picking up all the bits she could see. Noticing that she was so well pleased with this new building material, we added some more scraps and some tufts of cotton wool to the supply. Charmed with her good fortune, and grown bolder, the pretty creature ventured nearer to us and took all the scraps we chose to scatter for her on the grass.

The work of building went on so rapidly that in the course of two hours she had constructed a most delicate and dainty looking snow-white nest, and the pair took possession of this novel-looking house with festal song. But ah me! their joy was destined to be of but short duration.

"The best laid schemes o' mice and men
    Gang aft a-gley."[5]

and in the present case so it proved with our pair of little architects.

A heavy thunder-shower came on at noon of the next day. I leave my readers to imagine the result. The fairy-like palace, like all castles in the air, had collapsed, and, "like the baseless fabric of a vision, left but a wreck behind."[6] However, our brave little birdie cried, "Never say die!"[7] and set to work once more, made wiser by experience, building a more substantial nest in a lilac bush close by; but with a feminine weakness for finery she paid many visits to the frail ruin, selecting such of the more substantial materials among the rags as she found likely to prove useful in binding the walls of the new nest together, but not sufficient to weaken the more suitable articles which she wisely adopted for her work.

The new nest was an excellent specimen of skill, and the bits so judiciously woven in this time proved highly ornamental. I fancied the little builder felt proud of her work when it was finished, and we gave it unqualified praise.

The ruined tenement excited the admiration of a catbird.* She also had a taste for pretty soft bits of muslin and gay scraps of colored prints; so her ladyship set to work very diligently to repair the now dilapidated nest with the addition of dried fibrous roots, and grass, moss and all sorts of trash, which, with the rags, were soon wrought up into a substantial nest which formed the receptacle for five bluish-green eggs. But misfortune

---

*Galeoscoptes carolinen[s]is (Linn.).

seemed to cling to the coveted nest, for an accident, which might have ended fatally to the catbird, befell her one day. When about to leave the nest her legs became entangled in some loose strings which she had woven among the other materials, and, unable to free herself, she fell down head foremost into the midst of a rosebush, very stout and spiny, out of which she could not extricate herself, but lay fluttering and uttering the most doleful cries, more like the yells of an enraged cat than a bird.

The unusual outcry brought me to the rescue, and at my near approach she ceased her cries, and I truly believe the poor captive looked to me for help. I quickly perceived the cause of her disquiet, and with my scissors soon set her free. With a joyful cry she flew away, and, what seemed to me a remarkable proof of sagacity in the bird, she forsook the nest, never again venturing back to it, though it contained the five blue eggs. She evidently felt it better to forsake them unhatched than run any risk of danger to herself or her little brood. This, at any rate, was my own conclusion on the subject, though it may not have been that of the catbird.

While sitting on the eggs, and while the young ones are yet unfledged and helpless, the mother bird becomes bold and excitable. If anyone approaches too near to her nursery, she flies round the nest with outspread wings uttering strange angry cries, as if resenting the impertinent attempt to pry into her family affairs, and should the intruder venture closer she would no doubt punish him with strokes of her bill and wings.

The catbird belongs to the same family as the southern mockingbird,* and by many persons has been known by the name of "False Mockingbird."

It is a common idea that the note of the catbird is most discordant, like the mewing of an angry cat; but this is, I think, a mistake. The *true song* of the catbird is rich, full and melodious, more like that of the English thrush.† In point of fact, this bird is the best songster among the summer visitants in Canada.

I have fully satisfied myself that the harsh, wild squalling cry attributed to the parent birds is that of the young birds when the mother has forsaken them, leaving them to shift for themselves, and, like weaned children, the call is for food and companionship. This is my own observation from watching the birds.

Mimus polyglottos
†*Turdus melodius.*

ANOTHER MAY MORNING

"The birds around me hopped and played;
　　Their thoughts I cannot measure;
　　But the least motion which they made
　　It seemed a thrill of pleasure.

"The budding twigs spread out their fan
　　To catch the breezy air;
　　And I must think, do all I can,
　　That there was pleasure there."
　　　　　　　　　　　　—Wordsworth[1]

THIS morning, May 20th, I saw the first hummingbird of the season, later than usual.

A lovely living gem is the Ruby-throated Hummingbird,*[2] with its brilliant ruby, green and gold colors flashing in the sunlight. The rapidity of its flight is greater than that of any other bird. A dart and it is gone; we scarce can follow it with the eye. Sometimes it will fly in through an open

---

*Ruby-throated Hummingbird—*Trochilus Colubris* (*Linn.*). *Hab.*—Eastern North America to the Plains, north to the fur countries, and south, in winter, to Cuba and Veragua. *Nest*, a beautiful specimen of bird architecture, usually placed on the horizontal branch of a tree in the orchard, composed of grey lichens, lined with the softest plant down. *Eggs*, two, pure white, blushed with pink while fresh. McIlwraith, *Birds of Ontario*.

Hepatica, Bellwort, Spring Beauty, Anemone, by Agnes FitzGibbon,
in *Canadian Wild Flowers* (1868).

window, hover a moment over the flowers, cut or in pots, which have
attracted it, then dart away again into the sunshine. It is so delicate that
the least rough handling kills the lovely creature.

We are so late this year, the honeyed bells of the scarlet rock columbine
are not yet open. A few more sunny days and they will be out, and then the
hummingbird will have a feast. Meanwhile he is not starving, but is bus-
ied with the blossoms of the sugar maples in the grove outside my garden.

What a sight those maples present just now! The leaves are only beginning to burst from their brown winter sheathing, but the tassels of pale
yellow flowers hang pendent from every spray, dancing in the light warm
air; every breath sets the delicate thready stalks in motion, and the sunbeams brighten the flowers to gold against the blue of the May-day sky.

Truly the trees are a sight to gladden the eye and to lift up the rejoicing heart from earth to the throne of the glorious God who has given such beauty to His creatures to enjoy.

"Father of earth and heaven, all, all are Thine!
      The boundless tribes in ocean, air and plain;
      And nothing lives, and moves, and breathes in vain;
   Thou art their soul the impulse is divine!
   Nature lifts loud to Thee her happy voice,
      And calls her caverns to resound Thy praise;
      Thy name is heard amid her pathless ways,
   And e'en her senseless things in Thee rejoice.
   O God! what homage shall he pour to Thee,
   Whom Thou hast stamped with immortality!"
                                    —*Jane Roscoe*[3]

This is a sweet, quiet spot. The river, the bright, rapid Otonabee the Indian word for "flashing water running fast" lies at the foot of the grassy slope and open grove of forest trees which divide my garden from its shores. From the opposite bank the village cottages, church spires and busy factory cast their shadows on the stream.

There is a murmur of wheels and rushing rapids from below the mill dam, blended and softened to one harmonious monotone, ever singing the same tuneless song which soothes and never wearies on the ear.

'Tis pleasant to rest here in the sunshine and take in the quiet surroundings of the spot. I had nearly fallen asleep this warm morning, when I was roused by the joyous carolling of the wrens on the lattice of the veranda.

The mother bird is sitting, and her faithful mate comes to cheer his little wife with gay songs. He does not seem to heed me; he knows by experience that I am an old friend.

I have often thought that before sin marred the harmony of Nature the birds and animals were not afraid of man, but rejoiced in his presence: that Adam understood their language, and they knew his will, obeying the voice of their master. Now, all is changed. The timid and defenceless flee from man, as from an enemy. His presence awakens hatred and fear in the wild denizens of the forest, while the roar of the lion and the howl of the wolf inspire his dread. It was not so once, and there is a promise that the old harmony shall be restored, when "the earth shall be full of the knowledge of the Lord, as the waters cover the sea."[4]

Three summers ago a Black-billed Cuckoo* visited my garden and made her shallow nest of dried roots and hay on the flat branch of a white spruce, not more than six feet from the ground, so that she was easily seen as she sat within it.

I was attracted in passing the tree by the glitter of her large lustrous black eyes, and, on approaching nearer, by her soft rounded head, the snowy whiteness of her breast and her delicate fawn-brown back and wings. The silkiness of the plumage contrasted finely with the dark horny bill and full black eyes.

The shallow saucer-shaped nest was not large enough to contain the long tail, and it hung out beyond the edge.

I had never been so near to the cuckoo before, and was struck by the beauty of the bird and her wise ways.

On a movement of my head in order to get a closer peep at the pretty creature, she became alarmed and silently dropped off the nest backwards, slyly slipping out of sight among the grass and herbage below the tree; then, noiselessly gliding away, she reappeared on a tree beyond the garden and uttered a succession of loud angry cries, each a distinct syllable—"Kow! kow! kow! kow!"—repeating them many times, as if to say in threatening tones, "How dare you look into my nest, you big, disagreeable creature!"

That was what she meant; so, knowing I was an impertinent intruder, I retired to a little distance to allow her to return to her four beautiful pale blue eggs, pocketing the affront for the time, but often returning to take a furtive peep at Mistress Cuckoo and hear her scolding cry of "Kow! kow!"

I had hoped to make myself acquainted with the little brood, but unluckily the nest was discovered by some boys of bird-nesting propensities, or it may have been by a cat. In fact I had my suspicions that one or other of our own tomcats may have been the culprit that robbed the poor cuckoo of her eggs or newly hatched birds.

---

*Black-billed Cuckoo *Coccyzus Erythrophthalmus* (Wils.). *Hab.*—Eastern North America, from Labrador and Manitoba south to the West Indies and the valley of the Amazon; west to the Rocky Mountains. Accidental in the British Islands and Italy. *Nest*, loosely constructed of twigs, grass, strips of bark, leaves, etc. and placed in a bush. *Eggs*, two to five, light greenish-blue.—McIlwraith, *Birds of Ontario.*

The common name "Rain Crow" was given the Black-billed Cuckoo on account of her loud, oft-repeated note being heard before rain.

There is another bird belonging to the Cuckoo family that is common to North America and western or southern Ontario, but is not often seen to the north and east. This is the Yellow-billed Cuckoo (*Coccyzus Americanus*), a bird of quiet and retiring habits, seen generally in orchards and in groves on the banks of rivers.

May 21st.—Another lovely day. The air is full of sweet sounds and lovely sights. The young leaves are bursting on every spray of bush and tree.

Many of our wildflowers that did not come forth in their usual season, April, are now pushing out their blossoms as if in haste to meet the tardy warmth which has been so long withheld from the earth this year. I am glad to see them. Better late than never.

In the woods, under last year's sheltering bed of fallen leaves, they have bloomed because protected from the chilling winds; but here in the open borders of my garden they are late, very late. But why quarrel with the delay, since I now see the milk-white stars of the Bloodroot, so large and fine, gleaming brightly in the gay sunshine this May morning.

These beautiful flowers improve under cultivation, and are double the size of those in the grove close by.

The flowers of the sweet Liver-leaf (*Hepatica triloba* and *Hepatica rotundiflora*) are all out, a crowd of lovely starry blossoms of many hues—pink, blue, pale lilac and pure white. Delicate in scent, too, they are. The new spring leaves are unfolding, clothed with shining silk and shaded with a purplish cloud in the centre. They are already hiding the old withered and persistently clinging foliage of last year, throwing it off as a worn-out garment.

Here, late also, is the Spring Beauty (*Claytonia Virginica*), a frail and delicate flower. Its pink and white tinted and striped petals hardly look as if they could bear the cold breath of early April, but it is really hardy, and is not generally afraid of frost. This is, however, an exceptional season, or we should have seen the graceful Dog-tooth Violet (*Lilium erithronium*) showing its yellow drooping bells ere this date.

There is a large bed of these flowers just outside my garden, but they will not condescend to enter within cultivated ground, though I have often tried to coax the obstinate beauties to take root with me. They love their free-born liberty, and will have nothing to do with me and civilized life. They cling to the leaf mould, and the shade of the maples and beeches, and need the warm coverlet of scarlet and orange leaves the autumn winds spread over them; and perhaps—who shall deny it?—they may miss the companionship of grasses and ferns and mosses, or some native wildflower that mingles its roots and foliage among their own richly spotted leaves.

The name "Dog-tooth Violet," by which this fair lily is known, is surely a great misnomer. It has no affinity with the violet. The first part of the name has been derived from the white pointed bulb, which in color and shape is like the sharp canine tooth of a dog. "Dog-tooth Lily" we might tolerate as more correct or appropriate.

Baltimore Oriole, by Thomas McIlwraith, in *Birds of Ontario* (1894).

The wood ferns are all unrolling their fronds. The slender, delicate Maidenhair we call the "Fairy Fern" will soon be fluttering its tender leaflets like the young birds in the wood set free of the parent nest.

Just now a flash of glorious color darted past me, and I recognized at a glance the gorgeous plumage of the Baltimore Oriole—gold, scarlet-orange and purply black in varied contrasts. Beautiful is it beyond compare with any of our summer visitors, and among our native birds it has no peer.

The Baltimore is indeed "a thing of beauty and a joy forever."[5] Once seen it is never forgotten. How eagerly the eye follows its swift flight! But it is shy, and while we long for a second sight it is gone. It will not tarry to indulge us; it knows not the delight its presence gives us, and is hastening to join its mate. She, in her sober, modest dress of olive and brown, is no doubt as attractive in his eyes as he is to her in all his gay plumes of scarlet and gold.

The Indians, in their expressive language, call the Baltimore Oriole "Fire Bird," while the more prosaic settlers call it "Hang Bird," from its pendent nest, a name more fitting to its habits, but less poetical and descriptive of the bird itself than the Indian name.

The nest of the Oriole is a curious piece of workmanship, composed of all sorts of thready materials, picked up in all kinds of odd places, even in busy streets where no one would suppose so shy a bird would ever venture to appear.

I have in my possession a wonderful specimen of an Oriole's nest, taken from the branch of an acacia tree in front of a dry goods store in a busy, populous town. The nest is made of a mass of strings, pack thread, whip cord, cotton warp and woollen yarn. All these materials are most skilfully woven together in a regular network, and form a large soft elastic purse-shaped bag with a round opening in one side. The nest was suspended from the end of the bough by strings carefully fastened to it, and dangling from this curious hanging cradle is a long piece of string, to which is attached a large somewhat rusted packing needle, threaded, as if it had been used by the ingenious little worker in the manufacture of the bag, and there left. All the materials had been gathered up from the sweepings of the store, collected bit by bit, but at what time is a question unanswered.

So splendid a bird as the Baltimore Oriole picking up rags and odds and ends in a public thoroughfare one would think could hardly have escaped the eyes of men and boys, if done in noon-day; but there is a hidden wisdom possessed by God's little ones, and it strikes me that the work was done, and well done, too, in the early hours of the dawn. Before the earliest laborer was astir, going forth to his work, this little builder was busy at hers.[6]

The Baltimore is not the only bird that might be called a weaver. There are many foreign birds remarkable for their ingenuity in such work. The little Taylor Bird, which sews two leaves together as with a needle and thread, is one of these wonderful bird architects.

Here at my door is another of my little friends, the Chestnut-crowned Sparrow, of which I have already spoken in the preceding chapter. This familiar, social little bird is one of the earliest to make its appearance about our homes and gardens and is always welcome. It is as friendly in its ways as the dear robin used to be in the Old Country, and we reward it by treating it to crumbs from the table and any dainty little scraps that are at hand.

It is the very smallest of our birds—the smallest, I think, of all the many species of the sparrow family—and is so harmless and useful that it has many friends. A gentle, kindly little creature, it hops confidingly about our pathways and on the verandas, evidently in full confidence of being welcome at all times.

The name "Chipping Sparrow," which is often applied to it, arises from its weak note, "Chip, chip." Sometimes it raises a cheerful little attempt at a song, but the effort does not amount to much.

The reddish spot on its head is an unmistakable mark of the species. Its familiar, friendly habits distinguish this innocent little bird from any of the rest of the many sparrows that visit us during the breeding season, and we hail its arrival as among the earliest harbingers of spring.

> "They tell us that winter, cold winter, is past,
> And spring, lovely spring, is arriving at last."[7]

This tiny visitor comes before the swallow ventures to try her arrowy wings in the capricious air of our April weather. In bright sunny March days, while the snow is yet on the ground, its pleasant little note is heard, and it is often seen in company with the juncos, with which it associates in a friendly manner, the flocks mingling together in common, picking up seeds that lie scattered on the surface of the snow.

They are of wide distribution, being found all through eastern North America, beyond the Rocky Mountains westward, and even as far northerly as the Great Slave Lake. Its nest is simply constructed of fine dried grass, a few root fibres, cow's hair, and maybe a feather or two, built in some low bush near the ground. The eggs are a pale bluish green, three or four in number.

Another welcome friend is the Canadian Robin,* as he is commonly called: but he is only an immigrant. A few venture to winter with us, hidden, as we suppose, under the covert of the thick forest, but they are seldom seen.

Though he bears the familiar name of robin, he is not a real representative of the "household bird with the red stomacher," as one of our old divines[8] calls the English redbreast, yet the name serves to recall to the Canadian immigrant, in his far-off wilderness, the homely little bird that

---

*The American Robin—*Merula Migratoria* (Linn.).

so fearlessly entered open door or window as a familiar guest, loved and cherished by man, woman and child alike. The little bird that hops about their path and carols gaily at their side when all the other songsters are silent or have left for fairer climes and fruitful fields, holds a warm place in every heart.

The redbreast is held sacred: even the village boy, when out bird-nesting in grove or field, would not touch the nest of the sitting bird nor hurt the tiny fledglings. How often, as a child, have I heard the Suffolk distich from the lips of the country peasant boy:

"The robin and the chitty wren
  Are God Almighty's cock and hen"[9]

a rude rhyme, but spoken with reverence by the simple lad, and good in its teaching for the harmless bird's safety.

The American Robin is not a true thrush, but is a near relative to those sweet songsters, the Merle and the Mavis. He is one of the first of our early visitants. Before the snows of midwinter have quite melted, he comes across the St. Lawrence at different points, and spreads through the country on the lookout for a favorable settlement where he and his future spouse and family may make themselves a comfortable home for the long summer days to come.

The male birds come before the females, and in small parties, I think, as it is usual to see four or more of them near each other in the fields and gardens. It speaks well for the domestic harmony of their lives, this looking out for the future comfort of their partners, and a good example for our young men to follow before taking to themselves wives. Commend me to the wisdom of Mister Robin.

There is great rejoicing when the bevy of young females come over the borderland, followed by, I am sorry to say, a good deal of fighting before matrimonial arrangements are completed.

I rather think that our male robins help to construct the large unsightly nest, or at any rate assist in bringing the materials—sticks, roots, dried grass stalks, straw plastered with clay, not very neatly—in fact, it is about as fine as a chopper's shanty, rough and ready, but serves its purpose as a nursery *pro tem* for the young birds.

If we examine the nests of some of the smaller birds—the finches, for instance—and notice the beauty of structure, the smoothness of finish, the symmetry of form, the softness and delicacy of the interior—no roughness nor hardness in the material, all loose threads tucked in so neatly—and then think of the tools the little builders have had to work with, well may we be filled with admiration and astonishment.

Take the nest of the goldfinch, and then see what the little creature has at her command. Only a tiny awl-like bill, which must answer for knife or scissors to cut and clip her building material; the claws on two tiny feet, for though we do not know how she uses them, a great deal of the work must fall to their share; a soft rounded breast with which to mould and shape and smooth the cup-like structure till it acquires the exact circumference and size needed for the accommodation of five little eggs, and later on five little birds that are to be fed and cared for until such time as the parents judge they may be safely left to shift for themselves.

This nest is as perfect as if the most skilful hands and the most delicate fingers had put the finishing touches to it and the most critical artistic eyes had overlooked the building—if, indeed, any human skill could construct it, even with all the appliances of modern knowledge.

In most instances it is the female bird who takes upon herself the labor of building the nest. This is a labor of love, and the bird puts forth all the energies of her nature and all the skill with which she is inspired to accomplish her work well.

Having the stereotyped pattern ready, she seeks a suitable place and lays the foundation as any builder would do. She gathers material bit by bit, the strongest and most substantial first. She selects or rejects this or that, according to her plan and the order to be observed—wool that the thorns and bushes have caught from the sheep and lambs; hair that cow or horse has let fall; grey lichens picked from a wall, and tender green moss from a fallen tree. Taking here a bit and there a morsel, to give strength or elasticity, needful warmth or softness, she weaves all together according to the family pattern. Birds are very conservative, and deviate very little from the ancestral form or type of architecture.

Ah, here is one of Nature's mysteries! Who taught the little bird builder and upholsterer to use the same materials, to shape her nest (possibly the very first one) to the exact size and pattern, to line it inside just like the one her mother and all the goldfinch family had made centuries before she came into the world? So like is it that no country lad seeing it would ever mistake it for that of a robin or a blackbird or a yellowhammer, bearing, as it does, in its construction, the unmistakable trademark of this particular little architect.

Are not these things, simple as they may appear, worthy of our attention? May they not lead us from the nest of the little bird and her ways to the throne of the great All-wise God, who has implanted in His smallest creatures a wisdom that baffles the reason of the wisest of men to understand and explain? Truly

> "There are teachings in ocean, earth and air;
> The heavens the glory of God declare."[10]

Did not our Lord, in whom the fulness of wisdom dwelt, point out to His disciples lessons to be learned from the flowers of the field and the birds of the air?[11] We learn from them perfect obedience to His will and dependence on His care; unselfish devotion, from their care for their offspring; perseverance, forethought and industry, from their efforts in obtaining food for the sustenance of their helpless family; unity of purpose, from the gregarious birds who move in flocks actuated by one will in their flight to distant climes; order, discipline, and obedience to their leader, as in a well-drilled army on the march. Watch the movements of a flock of wild-fowl on the wing to some far-away breeding ground; there is discipline and prompt obedience, and evident plan and controlling power. We hear not the word of command, we know not the signals given, but we can see there is a ruling power regulating every change in the host, and that there are no rebels in the army.

MORE ABOUT MY FEATHERED FRIENDS

"Now out of woodland copse and cover,
    Dies the summer as died the spring,
And days of delight for lover and lover,
    And buds that blossom and birds that sing;
And southward over our inland seas
Have vanished the humming-bird and the bees;
Fleet on the blast the dead leaves hover;
    Loud in the forest the axe-strokes ring."
                              —*C.P. Mulvaney*[1]

THE PINE GROSBEAK

AMONG the few species of birds that linger in our cold climate in the shelter of the pine forests and cedar swamps, is the Pine Grosbeak (*Penicola Enucleator*).

Like the Crossbill (*Curvirostra*) he is a brave, hard fellow, and of a sociable nature. He is usually met with in parties of from five or six to eight; probably it is the *paterfamilias* who leads the flock, the spring or summer hatch.

In our winter gardens, and in groves where there are evergreens, balsam firs, spruce and cedars, the pine grosbeaks may be seen busily searching for seeds and insects, scattering showers from the dry cones they tear asunder, it may be, for the seeds or for the hidden larvae of the pine-destroying *Buprestians* with which many species of the cone-bearing trees are infested. The larch and spruce are destroyed by the larvae of the Sawfly, and the spruce particularly by the Bud moth.

The grosbeak is a handsome bird when in full plumage. The rich cin-namon-brown, varying in shades, of the females and young birds, though fine, is not comparable to the dark crimson, shaded to black, of the older male birds. In size the full-grown birds are as large, or nearly as large, as an English blackbird or thrush.

The thick bill marks the family of the grosbeaks, of which the English bullfinch also is one. This form of the bill is very well suited to the food of the bird, consisting as it does of hard nutty berries, juniper and red cedar, and the seeds of the cone-bearing trees. This seems to be more especially his winter bill of fare, for in the autumn the berries of the mountain ash are eagerly sought and evidently enjoyed.

THE SCARLET TANAGER

The Scarlet Tanager (*Piranga Erythromelas*) is another brilliant bird. The Indians and the old settlers in Canada call it the "War Bird," because, they say, it was not seen on this side of Lake Ontario, nor on the St. Lawrence, till after the close of the war between Great Britain and the United States, in 1812-14, not until peace was established.

The country, however, was but sparsely inhabited before that date, and it is probable there were not many among the settlers who would take much note of, or any particular interest in, the coming and going of the birds. Though much reliance cannot be placed on such traditions, yet one often chances to glean interesting facts from them. The old settlers in the bush and the Indians were my only sources of information about the birds when I first came to the Colony. The natural history of the Dominion had not then attracted the attention of writers to any extent.

To see this now rare bird, the Scarlet Tanager, one must go back into the lonely forest settlements, as he does not affect the vicinity of towns and villages, but loves the seclusion of the quiet woods, far from the noisy haunts of men. In the silent depths of the forest his nest is secure from the acquisitive boy and the prowling cat.

During my first year's residence in the Douro backwoods, I used to watch eagerly for the appearance of these beautiful scarlet birds. The black feathers of the wings and tail form a fine contrast to the bright plumage of the neck and back. As the woods are cleared away we lose many of our summer visitors from the other side of the lakes.

The tanager's nest is made of strips of bass and fine rootlets woven together and fastened securely to a branch where no rude winds can shake it. There they hatch their little broods, and, as soon as the young birds are fitted for the change, quietly depart, their dazzling robes being no more seen glancing among the dark shades of the forest. So peacefully do our "war birds" come and go.[2]

One day, some years ago, I met an Indian with a dead bird in his hand, which by its thick short bill I recognized as one of the grosbeak family, but unlike any of those birds I had before seen, the pale whitish plumage of its breast being dashed with crimson spots, just as if its throat had been cut and the drops of blood had fallen in an irregular shower on the breast.

I asked Indian Peter the name of the bird. With the customary prologue of "Ugh!" a guttural sort of expression, he replied, "Indian call bird 'cut-throat'; see him breast!" thus calling my attention to the singular red marks I had noticed, and at the same time showing me that they were not bloodstains caused in the killing of the bird. He was taking it to a young gentleman who wanted it as a specimen, and who was a clever taxidermist.

I could gain no further information from Peter, nor have I ever seen another specimen of the bird with this descriptive name. I have, however, since found in a lately published work, "The Birds of Ontario," by Thomas McIlwraith, already quoted, that the dress of the female grosbeak is a pale whitish-grey, and it strikes me that this may have been a hen-bird but partially colored, or a male bird not in full dress.

While speaking of my Indian friend Peter I recall a little scene which took place in the post office at Gore's Landing, at that time a general rendezvous for both busy folk and idlers. As is usual in country places, the office was also a store, and was kept by the gentleman before alluded to as a collector of birds, etc. The Indian hunters were his best customers, trading their furs and game for tobacco, groceries and other necessaries.

Peter was a picturesque figure as he marched into the store, gun in hand, and clad in his blanket-coat and red sash, especially as drawn through this red sash hung a beautiful Hawk-owl.*

Everyone exclaimed, "What a beauty!" but Peter taking it from his sash, flung it on the counter with a word that did not sound at all nice.

"Why, Peter!" said Major St. Q____, "what's the matter?"

"Ugh! Shoot no more hawk-owl, nor eagle; no more again. He like to kill me!"

Then, becoming a little less excited, he gave the history of his trouble in tolerably good English, for Peter was Indian only on the mother's side.

"I went out shoot something in woods for dinner. No partridge, no squirrel, no hare. See mister hawk-owl on branch in cedar swamp— shoot him. Guess William Brown here give me something good for hawk-owl. Stuff, you know. Pick him up, draw him through sash, carry him so. By and by hawk-owl, him not dead, him get

American Hawk Owl, by Thomas McIlwraith, in *Birds of Ontario* (1894).

alive again—stick him beak and claws in my back. By Jove, I sing out! Couldn't get beak out of my back-bone. I keep yell loud, till brother John he come. Hawk he hold on. No get him let go. John he say, 'Cut him's head off,' and it hard work then to get him beak out of my back. I swear, I never shoot hawk-owl, no, nor eagle, no more."

Poor Peter, I do not think he quite approved at first of the peals of laughter with which his story was received. It certainly was very droll and greatly diverted his unsympathetic auditors.

*American Hawk-owl—Surnia Ulula

However, Peter was comforted by a small gift and a plug of tobacco from the Major.

THE BLUEBIRD

As the redbreast is to the British Isles, so is the bluebird to the Americans. It is often spoken of as "Wilson's Bluebird,"[3] because of that ornithologist's partiality for it, and it is ever cherished and protected from wanton injury. It is, however, less frequently seen now in the inland settlements north of the great lakes than in former years.

Its song is varied, and its lovely cerulean blue color delights and charms the eye as it flits among the trees in our groves and gardens.

Its nest is placed low with us and is not very carefully concealed—so kindly is this sweet bird treated in its American home that it is unsuspicious of danger when paying its summer visits to us.

Mr. McIlwraith says that the immigrant English sparrows are to blame for the increasing rarity of the bluebirds' visits to their old haunts, and closes his charming book with a quotation from Wilson's lines in praise of his favorite bird.[4]

THE CANADA JAY*

If an Indian hound intrudes into the house, his master dismisses him with the words, "*Wis-ka-geen*," which mean, "Get out, lazy fellow," and the Indian name for that bold, troublesome bird, the Canada Jay, the pest of the lumberer's camp in the Northwest, is very similar, "*Wis-ka-Tjan*." This the Hudson Bay folks have turned into the more familiar sound of "Whiskey John" or "Whiskey Jack."

This daring bird comes of a doubtful race, not very distantly related to the jays, crows, magpies and some other noisy and not altogether reputable characters, and is himself a sort of freebooter, not famed for his strict regard for the rights of *meum* and *tuum*.[5] In the words of an old Hudson Bay trapper, he is "a nateral-born thief."

He is, indeed, a free-and-easy sort of fellow. When not stealing he is as full of idle mischief as a schoolboy, nor has he any beauty of appearance

---

*The Canada Jay—*Perisoreus Canadensis*. Indian name, *Wis-ka Tjan*—"Whiskey Jack."

to make up for his bad qualities.

My first acquaintance with these, to me, strange birds commenced at the house of my hospitable friends, the Stewarts, of Auburn, where I was always a welcome guest.[6]

On one occasion my husband and I were detained there for two days by a very heavy snow storm and subsequent high winds and deep drifts.

After breakfast Mr. Stewart opened a window which faced the river below the house, the rapid Otonabee, at that time bounded on the opposite shore by a dense forest.

Blue Jay, by Thomas McIlwraith, in *Birds of Ontario* (1894).

Immediately on a signal whistle being given, a pair of "whiskey jacks" flew across the river to the open window. Mr. Stewart had previously placed a small board with one end resting on the window sill and the other supported by the edge of the table, from which the breakfast dishes had not yet been removed. The board thus formed a bridge for the accommodation of the bold pair. Up they marched, and, like the little foxes,

"Very soon they were both at work,
　Waiting neither for knife nor fork."[7]

Potatoes, crumbs of bread and scraps of meat vanished quickly; bones were dexterously picked, nothing seemed to come amiss, and as soon as the feast was over away flew the "whiskey jacks," back to the shelter of the woods to preen their feathers as they sat on the grey branch of an old oak tree that stretched its leafless arms over the cold but still unfrozen waters of the river.

"These birds are as full of frolic as little children," said our host; "by and by they will be over again in the backyard picking up any bits they see and take a fancy to, chasing any article that may be blowing about in the wind and playing with it as any puppies would do."

While the birds had been enjoying their breakfast on the table, I had been taking notice of their plumage. It was of a dusky slate-grey, loosely set and hairy, the neck and head a shade darker, with a dirty yellowish white ring around the neck; there was some white, too, on the under part of the breast and tail. The latter was long and kept in constant motion, the bird, as he walked, flirting it up and down with a would-be careless air, which, together with the quick glancing, mischievous expression of the eye, gave a peculiar character to his countenance, and marked him as a bold, daring, yet sly, unscrupulous fellow, caring for nobody but his own audacious self.

I was so much amused by the sauciness of the pair of Northwesters, visitors from the far-off fur country of the Hudson Bay territories, or the northern parts of the Rocky Mountains, that I said to our host, "I wish these droll birds would pay our clearing a visit."

Mr. Stewart laughed, and said, "I'll send them up. Look out for them."

And, strange to say, the day after our return home, as if the cunning fellows had heard and understood what had passed, there they were hopping about at the back door, wagging their tails and picking among the newly swept snow and *débris* in their usual free and easy style.

Of course every attention was paid to our visitors in giving them food. They made many trips to the stable and barnyard, and having fully satisfied their curiosity and acquired a knowledge of the establishment, they came to the garden and there amused themselves with a piece of rag they had discovered somewhere about the premises, of which they made a fine plaything. They tore it into shreds, and carrying them to the garden fence, hung them on the pickets, turning and twisting them, tossing them to and fro, eyeing them from every point of view, with head on one side and their bright eyes twinkling as if with the very spirit of fun and mischief.

If the "whiskey jacks" did not enjoy their play, my little boy did. He laughed and clapped his hands with glee as he stood on a chair by the window and watched their pranks.

Whether our visitors preferred the abundant and varied fare they were accustomed to receive daily at the hospitable table at Auburn, or whether they were only on a visit, is a question we never solved, but they certainly disappeared early the following morning and returned to us no more.

Possibly our cat Nora had kept too watchful an eye on their movements or the great dog Nero had alarmed them, or it may be they preferred their favorite perch on the old oak tree by the river.

The fur trappers of the Northwest regard these jays as a great nuisance, as when pressed by hunger they damage the furs that are suspended in their tents or wigwams, as well as devour the jerked meat hung up to dry.

So bold are these feathered plunderers that it is in vain the men hurl all sorts of missiles at them; if driven off for one minute, back they come the next and pounce upon the meat as audaciously as ever.

"Nor is their flesh worth eating; it is mean stuff, and not worth powder and shot," said my informant, who evidently held the game in no small contempt.

THE RED-WINGED BLACKBIRD*

These birds are abundant in Canada, especially haunting the shores of the lakes and rivers though they are not water birds. They live chiefly on wild rice and the seeds of aquatic plants and insects, but are very troublesome to the farmer, as they make great havoc of his grain fields.

At night they roost on the trees and among the bushes at the borders of marshy places. About sundown they gather in great flocks and return to their leafy lodgings, filling the air with the noise of their wings, chattering and calling to each other.

They have their sentinels in the daytime to warn the flock of approaching danger. These utter a note which sounds like the words "Geek! geek!" often repeated. There is also another note uttered slowly like the twang of the string of a harp.

I used to listen for this vibrant note and try to discover its meaning. No doubt it was a signal to its comrades, as the flock would rise on the wing at once upon hearing it.

The feathers on the upper part of the wing of this bird give it the name of Red-wing. The gay shoulder knot, like a soldier's epaulette, brightens

*Agelaius Phoeniceus (Linn.).

and relieves the dead black of the plumage. When on the wing this bright spot is seen better, the light catching it as the birds wheel about, and giving a flash of color scarcely visible when they are at rest.

Nearly allied to our red-shouldered blackbird is the yellow-headed blackbird, a large handsome fellow with the whole head and upper portion of the breast and neck of a bright yellow.

This fine species is not common with us, but is sometimes met with in Ontario. He is the *Xanthocephalus* of Bonaparte,[8] and belongs rather to the Western States of America; eastward he is only an occasional visitor.

THE FISH-HAWK*

"The osprey sails above the Sound;
    The geese are gone, the gulls are flying;
The herring shoals swarm thick around,
    The nets are launched, the boats are plying.
Yo ho! my hearts! let's seek the deep,
    Raise high the song and cheerily wish her,
Still as the bending net we sweep,
    God bless the fish-hawk and the fisher."

—*Wilson*[9]

A bold fisher and a successful one is the Osprey, second only in his power of wing and keenness of vision to the rapacious Baldheaded Eagle, his great rival, who with lordly arrogance, acting on the ungenerous spirit of might overcoming right, often robs him of his lawful prey.

However, as both these birds are thieves and tyrants, we need not waste sympathy upon the Fish-hawk, especially as he in turn has none for the poor defenceless waterfowl. He pounces upon them while they are harmlessly disporting themselves on the pools of water just opened out between the masses of floating ice in the lake this warm April day. Happy creatures! They are heedless of the watchful eye of their enemy hovering above them, ready to descend with hooked beak and sharp talons upon the fairest and plumpest of the flock.

---

*The American Osprey—*Pandion Haliaetus Carolinensis*

Silly birds! Why don't they look up instead of enjoying their bath, or standing in groups on the edge of the ice, preening their feathers and indulging in idle gossip with their neighbors, or preparing themselves for a fresh plunge in the water, a luxury so long denied them by the rigors of winter?

There! What a wild commotion ensues when at last they become aware of the proximity of their enemy, as he makes a sudden descent and bears off a duck or a young goose in his terrible talons! How they rise *en masse* on clamorous wing and wheel and fly from his dread presence!

Possibly he might have preferred a bass or a perch, or a big sucker, had such a prize been more available, but "all is fish or fowl that comes to his net,"[10] and a delicate duck or gosling is not to be despised; so he is content with what he has taken, and flies off to some quieter spot, out of sight and hearing of the noisy crew he has outraged, to take his meal in thankfulness. The water fowl, meanwhile, pop down once more upon the bosom of the lake, and are soon flirting and splashing the sparkling water over back and wings as if no enemy had ever disturbed them or robbed them of one of their number.

THE BELTED KINGFISHER*

This bird visits Ontario in April or May, and may be seen on the banks of all the lonely lakes and rivers. It has not the brilliant plumage of the European bird, and is by no means as graceful in form. Its note is a very unpleasant one, a loud quick rattling cry uttered as it skims along the borders of lake or stream, a solitary object seeking its sustenance from the waters, or, it may be, procuring food for its young brood or the mother bird on the nest.

The dusky white ring about the neck is a marked feature in the bird. The bluish grey of the feathers is barred with black on the wings and tail; hence its name, "Belted Kingfisher." It builds no nest, but the female bird deposits her eggs in the enlarged end of a tunnel dug in a sandbank.

It stays late with us and does not seem to feel the cold. It is only when the frost has driven the fish to seek shelter in the deeper waters, and the belted bird can no longer obtain the requisite food, that he flies south.

Ceryle Alcyon (Linn.).

KINGBIRD*

The habits of the Kingbird are highly amusing to watch. He is about the size of a blackbird, of dusky plumage, but with a white border to his tail and some white in the edges of the wing feathers. His note is very harsh and grating, and his favorite position the top of any upright stick or bare pole, from which point of vantage he can survey the "limit" he has chosen to reign over. Here he sits turning his head until the bright glancing eye lights on some unwary insect; when he darts off and rarely misses his aim. His prey secured, he returns to his perch and awaits another chance.

Both names given him are descriptive, the latter apparently with good cause, if one may judge by the enmity shown him by all the smaller birds. They show this dislike by uniting together and making common cause against the enemy, attacking him, not in fair fight with beak and claws, but by keeping a certain distance above him and darting down and striking him on the head, then rising again swiftly to be ready to deal a second blow. The bewildered bird, unable to defend himself, can only flee from his tormentors and hide away among the thickest evergreens, fairly beaten out of the field.

Union is power; by it the weak confound the strong. Many an instance have I seen of a similar kind, many a big crow being forced to flee before the attacks of small birds. Even the hen hawk or harrier has been driven away by the united attacks of apparently insignificant but determined parties of two, three or four brave little creatures, whose plan was simply to keep above the head of their enemy, and out of his reach after striking their blows.

The swallow and martin are renowned for those feats of bravery. They are always victors, and might be crowned as champions of the helpless little songbirds who so often fall victims to the crow, the Kingbird and the hawk.

THE BOHEMIAN WAXWING

Another noisy crew are those pretty, wild pilferers of the garden and orchards, the cedar birds, or cherry birds, and names common to the smaller species of *Ampelidae*, or Waxwings.

---

*Tyrant Flycatcher—*Tyrannus*.

The larger, handsomer and more remarkable of the family is known as the Bohemian Waxwing, or *Ampelis garrulus*, and he is indeed a noisy, chattering fellow. These are not so common as the smaller cedar birds, but they occasionally visit us in large parties, and doubtless receive scant welcome from the market gardener, who does not approve of their brigandish assaults on his ripening cherries and other fruits. We, however, are more tolerant, and overlook their predatory habits in our amusement at their wild merry ways.

This morning there is a flock of some dozen individuals in my garden. They are full of frolic and fun, and if one may judge by the noise they are making as they fly hither and thither from bough to bough and tree to tree, they are having a gay time chattering and whispering to one another, and one might almost say, laughing, like a party of light-hearted children at play.

One wonders what it is all about. I really think it must be a wedding party, and a joyous one, too—a match of which both families approve. See how important some of the older birds look, setting up their soft-crested heads and puffing out their breasts. As they dart past me I catch sight of the bright scarlet ornaments, like bits of red sealing-wax, on the wing feathers. These jewels are the distinguishing marks of the full-grown male bird, and no doubt but the little feathered dandy is as proud of these bits of finery as any girl is of her brooches and bangles.

The Bohemian Waxwing is of foreign extraction. He is a little aristocrat, somewhat exclusive, and vain of the family of which he is the head. He does not mix himself up with the common folk, but keeps religiously to himself, for you never find him and his party with the smaller species, the cedar birds, native to the country.

The Bohemian is a great traveller, and seems to spend his time in visiting strange lands. He is found in many countries, and it is not easy to locate his home. He and his family do not settle down soberly, as some other birds do, but go where they please, stay awhile and then disappear, and you do not meet with them again for several seasons.

Besides the gay ornaments of the wing, the tail feathers are finely fringed with golden yellow, which is seen most distinctly when the bird is on the wing.

The berries of the mountain ash and the chokecherry (and, in winter, the fruit of the red cedar and juniper), form the food of these birds, with what ripe fruit the garden affords them; but if they eat the fruit they also destroy swarms of destructive insects.

The cedar bird is accused of destroying the buds of the apple trees, but in all probability this is a mistake. It may be only the hidden larvae of the codlin[g] moth, the curculio, the beetle, or fly, that is doing the real injury, depositing its eggs in the bud; and the cedar bird in seeking it as his prey is doing much good service in the orchard.

Man in his greed is often very short-sighted in his judgments.

THE ENGLISH SPARROW: A DEFENCE

"And He that doth the ravens feed,
   Yea, providently caters for the sparrow,
   Be comfort to my age."
                                   —*Shakespeare*[1]

Harmless, persecuted, despised, reviled sparrows, who is brave enough
to take your part? Who will take you under a sheltering wing and say a
word in your behalf?[2]

I dare so to do, setting at nought the torrent of invective which is sure
to fall on my defenceless head.

It was "Don't Care, that came to the lions." So ran the awful warning
for wilful folk that I used to pore over with childish credulity in Doctor
Fenning's Spelling Book, an ancient volume out of which I learned my
first lessons, and where villainous type, hideous pictures, bad paper, and
the use of *f* for *s* puzzled the brain and confused the eyes of the little
scholar of three years of age.[3]

Well, I "don't care" if I do come to the lions, I will have my say about
those poor sparrows, remembering the words of the gracious Lord, "Not
one of them shall fall on the ground without your Father."[4]

"Doth God take care for oxen?"[5] saith the apostle. Yea, He careth; yea,
and for the birds of the air also. He openeth His hand and feedeth them.

Not one—not even the sparrow, despised among thoughtless men—is forgotten by the great Creator,

> "Who sees with equal eye, as God of all,
>   A hero perish, or a sparrow fall,
>   Atoms or systems into ruin hurled,
>   And now a bubble burst, and now a world."[6]

There is a war of extermination against these birds going on in the Northwest, and among the farmers and gardeners in country places. A regular hue and cry is being raised for their destruction, and nowhere are they to be shown mercy.

Now, I would fain take their case in hand and endeavor to prove that this wholesale persecution is both unjust and unreasonable.

In the first place, were not the birds first brought into the country through avarice or ignorance, as a speculation, by some adventurous Yankee, who "assisted"[7] them across the Atlantic in order to make merchandise of them?

Were they not introduced into the agricultural districts as destroyers of the weevil, army worm and all other kinds of injurious insects?

Yet it was very well known that the sparrow was a granivorous, and indeed an omnivorous bird. He is not dainty; he will take anything and every thing that falls in his way. As *paterfamilias* he is a good provider for his numerous offspring. Small blame to him! Sparrows and their young must live, they will not starve.

Yes, the sparrows will eat grain, and the farmer says they *do* eat the wheat, and therefore they must be killed.

But stop a minute. When do they eat the wheat? Only in the season, and that a very short one, of the ripening grain, as it is only then that they can get it, and when, with many other grain-eating birds, the sparrows flock to the harvest to take their share.

"Audacious robbers!" the farmer calls them, and straightway all the blame of his loss is laid on the immigrant sparrows. He forgets that the sparrows have been cultivating the crop, too, in eating and destroying the numerous insects that infest it while it has been in the blade and in flower, and does not stop to consider that the laborer is worthy of his hire.[8] The sparrow but takes his due for service unseen and unrecognized by the master of the field. Then when the crop is garnered, he is but one of the many gleaners who are busy for awhile in picking up the fallen wheat kernels scattered by the reapers.

The harvest and the gleaning season over, let us follow the sparrows to the villages and towns. There are here no fields of ripe grain to make havoc of, no farmers to offend, but the birds must be fed. How?

Look down on your streets and thoroughfares. On every heap of refuse, every scrap of garbage, in every dirty gutter or dropping in the roadway, about the sweepings from yard or store, are groups of these despised birds, busy, hard-working and unpaid scavengers.

Who knows what evils they prevent, what they devour that otherwise would become decayed vegetable matter, decomposed and typhoid-breeding filth; the larvae of beetles and other noxious insects, half-digested grain that if left would shortly breed corruption and disease hurtful alike to man and beast.

True, the birds are bold. The sparrow takes possession of the eaves and cornices of your buildings, your sign boards and your window sills. Any projecting beam or odd angle he makes his coign of vantage from whence to spy out what he wants. But in this he really interferes with no one, and it is only the braggart assurance of his manner that excites our aversion. His ragged nests are usually hidden away in out of sight corners or sheds, so we have not that to cite against him.

Ah! but someone comes down on me with the accusation that the cruel, wicked, malicious and altogether disreputable sparrow kills and drives away all our dear little songbirds.

Wait a bit, my good friend. Did the other birds never fight or attack strangers? The bill and claws of the sparrow are not those of the *Raptores*. He may be pugnacious, but so is our dear pet the redbreast.

"Fair fight and no favor," say I. Fight? Yes, they all fight at times, robin against robin, when they are in the humor for it, and the weakest goes to the wall.[9]

As to the accusation that the sparrows drive away other birds, let the other birds defend themselves. In physical strength they are all his equals.

I cannot help thinking, however, that it is a fact yet lacking confirmation. There is an old saying, "Give a dog a bad name and of course he suffers for it."[10] It is my impression that in this instance it is but a newspaper scandal got up for "copy," and endorsed by the farmers who first *introduced* and then *traduced* the poor sparrows; used them first to get rid of the pests that blighted their grain, then abused them for helping themselves to the wages begrudged them.

I have here the testimony of a very intelligent observer of Nature, one who has carefully watched the habits, food and peculiar ways of the sparrows in this country as well as in England. He says: "I have never been able to detect wheat or any other hard grain in the crop, and it is my opinion that these birds are more insectivorous that granivorous, and that it is the larvae of insects that they obtain in the buds of the fruit trees and in the ears and joints of the wheat and oats which induces their visits to the fields; and if they pick the husks it is not for the kernel itself, but for what is really destroying it. The sharp pointed bill of the sparrow is more suited for picking worms than taking up hard grain."[11]

To sum up, the sparrow, an invited guest, an assisted immigrant, was at first welcomed; then, when he had done the work required of him, we find he has other qualities for which we gave no contract, consequently we would like to assist him home again or exterminate him, as one who has outworn his welcome.

Though he betrays no secrets, he is an eavesdropper of the worst description. He makes holes in our eaves, and scatters the straw about, and is a nuisance; yet, on the other hand, he is a good scavenger and helps to keep the air about the house pure.

He is a bold, impertinent fellow who is always at hand to eat up the crumbs thrown out for his betters, and moreover he labors under the imputation of driving away other birds of more value in our eyes, but is known to be possessed of no more superior powers than they are provided with.

Thus the two heaviest counts in the indictment are: First, the destruction of grain; second, the driving away of the smaller and more valuable birds—both of which indictments have been pleaded by counsel as not proven.

Have I made out a good case for the sparrows? I have said my say. I am only a old woman after all, with a Briton's love of fair play, so let us give the poor sparrow a chance.

NOTES FROM MY OLD DIARY

"What atom forms of insect life appear!
And who can follow Nature's pencil here?
Their wings with azure, green and purple gloss'd,
Studded with colored eyes, with gems embossed;
Inlaid with pearl, and marked with various stains
Of lovely crimson, through their dusky veins."
—*Anne Letitia Barbauld*[1]

ON LOOKING over my old diary of a far-off date, 1839, I find notes of many things that struck me in the first years of my sojourn in my forest home —objects that then were new and interesting to me, but which now I seldom or never see.

There is a change in the country; many of the plants and birds and wild creatures, common once, have disappeared entirely before the march of civilization. As the woods which shelter them are cleared away, they retire to the lonely forest haunts still left, where they may remain unmolested and unseen till again driven back by the advance of man upon the scene.

It is rarely now that I catch a passing glimpse of the lovely plumed crossbill, or the scarlet tanager; seldom do I hear the cry of the bobolink, or watch the sailing of the baldheaded eagle or the fish-hawk over the lake, as I did formerly in fear for the safety of my little goslings. Even the gay, cheerful note of the chickadee is rarely heard, or the sonorous rapping of the red-headed woodpecker, or the plaintive, oft-repeated monosyllable of the wood phoebe.

I think these birds dislike the appearance of the red brick houses of the modern villages and towns, with their green blinds and fancy work in wood and paint. Perhaps they look upon them as possible traps to cage them, and find the old familiar rude shanty or log house more to their taste in architecture.

Here is one of my old notes made in that long ago time on the great cat-owl:

A very solemn, formidable-looking bird is this big long-eared owl. One was shot and brought into the house for my inspection. It was still living, having only been winged, and evidently was very angry with its captor, ready to avenge itself by a blow with its strong hooked beak and sharp talons. The glassy round eyes were glaring ominously from beneath the swathe of thick rich brown mottled feathers that half shaded them from the light. The ears, or the tuft of feathers that concealed them, stood up, giving a warrior-like aspect to the grand, proud bird.

Who is there among the early settlers that has not heard in the deep stillness of night, from some old oak in the woods or outbuilding near the house, the deep sonorous voice of the cat-owl calling to its mate? The hollow notes sound like "Ho-ho-ho-ho-," repeated with a pause between each syllable, as if to prolong the echo.

The Indian notes of lamentation over the dead, "*Wo-ho-ha-no-min*," seem an imitation of the mournful cry of this night bird.

An old Irish settler in the backwoods once gravely assured me that the "Banshee,"[2] the warning spirit of death or trouble which, he said, belonged to his family when he lived in Ireland, had followed him and his house to Canada. I looked a little doubtful. The old man grew angry because I asked:

"Did she come out in the ship with you?"

"Shure an' why should she not?" he replied. "Did she not cry all the time me poor wife—God rest her sowl—was in the death thraws? An' did she not cry the night the cow died?"

That indeed was a proof not to be doubted, so I judiciously held my

Irish Emigrant, Dennis O'Brien, on board the Cambridge,
Liverpool to New York, July 1844, by Titus Hibbert Ware.

sceptical tongue, though I thought it might well have been the cat-owl crying to her mate from an old hollow tree near the shanty; but it would have
been rank heresy to liken a real faithful family "Cry-by-night," or "Banshee" to a cat-owl.

Later the old man in rather an aggrieved tone, questioned my faith in the
"little people," or the fairies. When I suggested it was a long way for them
to come across the Atlantic, he took great pains to convince me that if they
cared for the family when they lived in Ireland, they would not mind how
long the voyage or the distance, so that they could watch over them here.

On the borders of the lake I see many beautiful dragonflies of all colors—red, blue, green, bronze, and some rare large flies with jet-black gauzy wings.

One kind, that I have tried in vain to capture, had a scarlet crescent mark on each lower pair of wings. Another, not less remarkable, was distinguished by azure blue crescents on the wings. These flies led me a chase for some time, I was so much struck with the beauty of the rare insects. They did not resemble the gay dragonflies in form or color, and I wished to obtain a specimen to send home to a friend; but after that summer I saw them no more, they having disappeared with the pine woods.

There is a pretty and curious insect, one of the Sphinx family, that comes out in the cool of the evening, and is very busy on the mignonette and other low growing border plants. It is very much like a bee in appearance, and sings a low humming song as it darts from flower to flower. Its body is longer and narrower than that of the bee, and its colors are black and white in bands. The lower wings of these curious moths are exceedingly small, the upper ones long and narrow. The swiftness of its hovering motions and the noise of its wings remind one of the hummingbird, hence people call it the Humming Moth.

The most beautiful of our native moths, and also the largest, is the exquisite pale green *Attacus luna*. This classical name was given it from the moon-shaped figure on each wing, showing the bright colors of blue and scarlet in the centre of the eye-like spots.

The lower pair of wings are lengthened into long tails like the schoolboy's kite, and are beautifully fringed with a pale gold bordering. These long tails are said to be of essential service in aiding the flight of the moth, serving to maintain a proper balance in its passage through the air. Several of our butterflies—as, for example, *Papilio turnus*, the handsome sulphur-colored Swallowtail—have this form in a great degree, while in others it is absent, as in *Danais archippus*, a fine red butterfly, one of our largest and most showy; also in the representative of the Camberwell Beauty and some others.

The body of the beautiful green *Attacus luna* is thickly clothed with soft silky white down. The legs, feet and antennae are of a coppery-red color, the latter short and finely pectinated—that is, having fine tooth-like projections.

The scarlet and blue colors are very effective in contrast to the exquisite tint of pale green which distinguishes this lovely moth from all others. It is very rarely to be seen now, but seems to love the shade among the orchard and forest trees.

It is in the orchard that we find the cocoons of that grand moth, the *Attacus cecropia*, a splendid insect, both in size, form and rich colors; as large, when its wings are fully expanded, as some of our smaller birds, measuring, indeed, nearly seven inches in width.

The heavy thick body of this insect is red, but marked by deep rings, and the surface clothed with soft whitish hairs. The head is large and the antennae strongly pectinated.

The marks on the wings are in the form of half moons, showing a variety of shadings, with vivid blue and some red in the centre. There are other lines and wavy marks on the wings, besides a deep rich border pattern.

I am afraid my very unscientific mode of description may offend the learned entomologist. If so, I crave pardon and plead limited knowledge as my sufficient excuse.

The common name for this fine moth is the Apple Tree or Orchard Moth, because its brown felted chrysalid cases are found attached to the twigs of orchard trees.

The first really hot days cause the imprisoned insect to burst from its sealed coffin, and its wonderful and mysterious resurrection to light and life is at once effected. It flutters forth a glorious but short-lived creature, perfect in all its beauty, to soar aloft in the sunlight and enjoy the sweet warm summer air for a brief season—a type to man of the promised resurrection of his own body from the dust of the earth, through the perfect work of redeeming love in the Lord Jesus Christ. "O Death! where is thy sting? O Grave! where is thy victory?"[3]

Since the above description of the *Attacus cecropia* was written, some years ago, I have had knowledge of two varieties of this remarkable beautiful moth.

About two years ago a friend sent me from Chicago three cocoons of this species. These cases, attached to slender twigs, were much smaller in size than the apple-tree variety, and were light brown and finely felted.

The moths (two came out all right, one was abortive) were smaller in every way, but beautiful in markings and color. They remained on a sunny window for some days, then one died and the other disappeared.

Last Christmas I was given another cocoon, fixed to a red-barked dogwood spray. It was of large size and very unlike the brown woolly cases I had hitherto seen. It was constructed of dead leaves and a grey papery substance like that of the wasp. There was no opening whatever in it; all was closely sealed up.

One sunny morning (April 21st) I was delighted at the sight of the tenant of the grey house, a magnificent specimen of the *Attacus* moth. It stood opening and closing its wings as if for flight, but remained for hours on the leaf of a scarlet geranium near the window, giving me a good opportunity of noting its beauty. Especially did I admire the rich coloring and markings on the wide wings, which were about six inches in extent and elegantly rounded and lobed.

The general color or groundwork was a rich dark red brown, with two large irregular white circular figures; within the larger circle was another figure semi-circular in form and of several shaded colors. The lower pair of wings were adorned in the same way, the edges being more scalloped and smaller than those of the upper wings, and beautifully marked and fringed with a bordering of white, red and grey.

The body of the moth was short and thick, barred with white, and having deep red spots between the lines. The outer surface of the back, seen between the open wings, was deep red. The legs were clothed with a velvety red down.

As soon as the lamp was lighted, the moth spread its wings and, bat-like, flew to the light, and would have been seriously injured had we not come to the rescue—not, however, before the feathery margin of the wings was somewhat scorched. Taken out of the room it flew about, casting a dark bat-like shadow on the ceiling. For some days it hid itself among the window curtains, coming out of this retreat only at night, and for the past few days it has remained fixed to the corner of the whatnot in the parlor. Its wings are closed, and it has apparently lost all its energy; the light no longer attracts it, the fine red pectinated antennae no longer are moved as at first—the beautiful creature is dead, or dying.

On a minute inspection being made of the empty cocoon, it seemed a mystery how the big, bulky insect could have escaped from its prison.

There was no visible aperture for its exit save one small pipe terminating in a tiny orifice, through which it seemed impossible that even the head of the creature could have issued. Yet, this must have been its door of egress, for no other was to be seen.

Among the myriad marvels in Nature, there are not greater than those found in the insect world.

I was given two of the large brown cases of the Orchard Moth last winter. I laid them aside in the drawing-room and forgot all about them. One warm May day, on going into the room, great was my surprise and delight to see two beautiful creatures on the window panes, enjoying the sunshine, and, I dare say, longing to be out in the warm free air.

By and by they became very restless, as if bewildered by the novelty of their surroundings, flitting about on the gay flowers of the curtains, and finally, after several days had elapsed one of the two deposited sixteen gold-colored eggs on the chintz. I make a note of the bare fact, and leave it to be pondered over by the experienced naturalist.

Besides the butterflies I have noticed in my old diary, I might have named the Tortoise-shell and the two Admirals, the red-marked one and the white. There are many others, too, which resemble in color and appearance species I was familiar with when in England.

There are the Tiger Moths, bright, gay creatures that come in at night attracted by the light of the lamp; and some large beautiful grey and rose-colored varieties with damasked wings, which shun the glare of the light and retreat to shaded corners of the walls out of sight.

Our beautiful oak trees are often disfigured when in full leaf by branches of brown or withered leaves, as if some scorching blast had fallen upon them.

I was standing on the lawn at my friends, the Haywards, admiring the glossy foliage of a group of handsome scarlet oaks (*Rabra coccinea*), one of the most beautiful of our native oaks, when my attention was drawn to one of the branches of a fine young tree near me which was affected by a quivering motion, while all the rest were quite still.

It was an intensely hot July day, not a breath of air stirring the leaves. Suddenly the branch parted from the tree and fell at my feet. I took it up to examine the cause of its fall. The leaves were still green and fresh, but on close inspection of the severed part, which was nearly half an inch in diameter, I found it finely grooved, as if it had been sawed or filed by some sharp toothed instrument.

This was evidently the work of a Sawyer or Borer, one of the numerous species of the destructive *Bup[r]estriœ,* which in the larvae state are so injurious to our forest trees.

I sought diligently on the ground for the little workman, but while I had been examining the branch he had hidden himself away in the grass, there to undergo the last change to the perfect state of his kind as a small beetle.

Being desirous of obtaining some information concerning the creature and its work, I turned to the report of the "Field Naturalists' Society of Ottawa"[4] for 1884 (page 49), and the following description satisfied me that my sawyer must have been the larvae of a Twig-girdler:

"*Oncideres cingulatus.* When the female desires to deposit her eggs she makes punctures in the bark of small twigs or branches. She then girdles the branch by gnawing a ring round it, which kills the branch, and in course of time it breaks off from the tree and falls to the ground, and the larvae feed on the dead wood. The beetle is greyish brown with a broad grey band. It is commonly known as the 'Twig-girdler.' "

In the present instance the leaf of the branch was still fresh and green, but at the same time I noticed the noiseless fall of branches from the oak trees adjoining, and saw that the ground was strewn with dead withered boughs and sprays, while others still hung by tiny shreds of bark, ready to fall, and disfiguring the appearance of the trees.

The entomologists now employed by the Government and attached to the Bureau of Agriculture, have of late years turned their attention to the appearance and habits of this class of tree-destroying insects, which are doing so much injury to the forests and orchards of the country.

The ravages of the various species of *Scaraboei* are not confined to the oak and pine alone, but every species of hardwood tree nurtures one or several kinds peculiar to itself.

The subject is one of considerable importance, and should not be devoid of interest even to the youngest student of natural history. It is a study particularly recommended to the agriculturist, horticulturist and florist, and it would be well if there were textbooks written in simple, plain language, that would be instructive and at the same time awaken an interest in it among our young people.

The habit of close observation inculcated and encouraged in children is a continual source of pleasure and profit in afterlife, often, indeed, leading to results that are little anticipated, as in the well-known case of Sir Isaac Newton, who had learned to see and think as a child—results so wonderful that the less observant have been disposed to attribute them to actual inspiration from God. True, He implanted the seed thus nurtured in the child, and brought forth the fruits in the man.[5]

But I am wandering away from my subject, the ways of those tiny insects, the twig-borers.

How marvellous and wonderful is their instinct! Note the curious means employed to accomplish an end which could not be foreknown by experience, by teaching or by reasoning, in the creature working for the future preservation of her unseen offspring. The calculating of the exact date when it should come forth, and the corresponding time when the girdled branch should part from the tree, thus providing a nursery for her infant and sufficient nutriment to sustain it, until in its turn it arrives at the perfect state of the mother beetle, to enjoy like her a brief term of life, prepare a cradle for its offspring, and die.

Surely this leaves a lesson for man to ponder over and confess that he knows but little. The wisdom of man must be but foolishness in the sight of God, since he cannot fathom even the ways of one of the most insignificant of the works of the Creator. How then can man by his puny wisdom find out God?

THE SPIDER

꒰꒱

"The spider taketh hold with her hands, and is in kings' palaces."
—Prov. xxx. *28.*[1]

I MUST confess to a natural aversion to spiders, an aversion I cannot over-come sufficiently to avoid shrinking from contact with them; yet I acknowledge that they are more interesting to me than any other of the insect tribe. I study their habits and ways with keener pleasure than I do those of the industrious bee or the active ant.

There is an individuality in the character of every spider which, in com-paring one with another and studying the peculiarities of each, gives it additional charm. Each spider appears to act independently of his fellows, and often indeed of the family pattern. He is not of a sociable nature, and though he will sometimes allow a small brother to give him a little help, or to look on when some large web is in hand, he more frequently carries on the work in an independent style, as if he were saying:

"Let me alone, if you please; I want none of your help. You only both-er me and run in my way. I have all my wits about me, my own tools and my own materials. I can mind my own business, and want neither your advice nor your assistance."

He is a surly fellow, a misanthrope, and a very ugly tempered as well as conceited one at that.

The spider certainly is accredited with possessing a very ferocious temperament, the males often fighting with great fury. The females, who are larger than the males, are even more combative—indeed the ungentle spouse is not infrequently charged with devouring her own husband! It is possible, though, that the victim may have been the meddlesome proprietor of a neighboring web, whose interference had aggravated her beyond endurance, and the act, therefore, might be termed justifiable *spidericide*.

Ugly and repulsive as some spiders are, they no doubt are as proud of their personal appearance as of their skill in the manufacture of the delicate webs which they hang out to lure unwary flies to their destruction, and so supply their pantries with the dainties they love.

But, seriously, what a marvel he is, what striking characteristics he has, what forethought, what vigilance. How clever are his contrivances and expedients wherewith to compass his desired end. Who can have failed to note his subtlety in concealing himself, his fierce and jealous temper— all traits belonging to the savage, and, alas, too often to be found among the more civilized of the human race.

But the spider is not altogether without his good qualities. We must do him justice, and not slay him without mercy.

He has energy, industry and great perseverance under difficulties. He is no idler. Instead of giving up immediately on the first failure, he sets to work to repair what has been destroyed or injured, not once but several times.[2] He is courageous, for he will not be daunted even by a wasp or a big blustering bully of a blowfly, twice as strong as himself; though, and this is hardly to be recommended as a good quality, he often overcomes his enemy by effective cunning. He has no pity for his victim, but casts his entangling threads over him and binds him down securely; then, knowing that his cries will bring him no aid and his struggles will but bind his bonds more closely and finally exhaust him, the wicked spider retreats to his dark corner and waits for the death of the unhappy prisoner.

An ugly picture! We will turn away from it now and see if we cannot find a more pleasant side to spider life in the maternal instinct.

One motherly spider carries her eggs along in a white silken bag wherever she goes, as if she were afraid to let them out of her sight. This is a dusky brown or black spider, and her greatest merit is the tender care she takes of her embryo, unhatched family.

There is another species, known by Old Country folks as the "Nursing Spider." She also carries her precious eggs in a fine yellow silk pouch, attached to herself by strings. The load is so nicely balanced that she can move quickly about without being in the least incommoded by it.

When the tiny things are hatched they follow their mother in a long train, each fastened to her by a silken thread. Where she goes, they go. They are of a bright reddish color and are very lively.

The old mother is by no means a disagreeable-looking creature; her body is about the size of a small garden pea, of a light yellow brown color.

It used to be a great source of amusement to me to watch the motherly care this amiable spider took of her numerous family when travelling over the flower borders. If one of them lagged behind or seemed disorderly, she came to a halt till they all assumed the regular marching position. What the word of command was, who could tell? But however it was given, it had the desired effect of restoring order.

A few years ago, when camping out with a party of friends on a picturesque and rocky island in Lovesick Lake, while the younger members of our party were bathing, I used to ramble along the rocky margin of the lake to look for ferns, fresh water shells and other curiosities.

One morning my eye was attracted by a ball of yellowish silk hanging in the middle of a soft maple bush, growing in the clefts of a fissure in the limestone rock.

The ball was about the size of a pigeon's egg, and was held in its place by a number of strong lines. On touching one of these with my finger, out rushed some dozens of small spiders, and from the bottom of the bush, to which several of the threads were attached, came a large black spider of formidable appearance and unusual fierceness of aspect.

Up she hurried to the rescue of her brood, examining the nest and lines with great care. Finding nothing injured in the cradle-bed and its fastenings, she ordered the frightened little ones back to their nest, and as soon as she saw them safely housed, retired slowly to her post at the foot of the bush. This time, however, she took the precaution to place herself facing the ball and its contents, that she might better keep a vigilant outlook for the enemy.

I confess that curiosity tempted me to renew the attack just to see what the mother would do, so I again touched one of the strings. The vibration was communicated to the mother as the little spiders again ran out, which instantly had the effect of bringing her up to their help.

How carefully she again sought to discover the cause of the trouble, her angry countenance showing manifest displeasure at the annoyance I had caused.

Upon nearer observation I perceived that a thread was attached to each one of the little creatures, and this again to the centre of the web, so that when they ran out, they formed a circle, and the movement caused a connecting thread or threads to convey the intelligence to the mother below.

I could not but admire the care and wonder at the marvellous instinct of maternity implanted as strongly in this little insect's breast as it is in that of any human mother. Truly instinct has been beautifully defined as "God's gift to the weak."[3]

There is a small, nimble species of field spider, with a black shining body, that is very numerous in rocky pastures.

Having first prepared a bed of some glutinous substance, she spreads it in a thin plate less in size than a three-cent piece. On this the eggs are deposited in due order, and over them is laid with great care and neatness a circular cover or lid which is made to fit as exactly as a pastrycook would cover a mince pie or oyster patty.

So artistically is our little spider pie finished, and the edges brought together so exactly, that one would think it had been pared evenly with a sharp knife and pressed closely to prevent prying eyes from discovering the baby spiders tucked in so carefully.

My little boy used to call them "little silver pies." Great was the astonishment of the child one day, when on raising the edge of one of these little cases out ran at least a dozen tiny black spiders.

What became of the family thus turned out of a house and home I do not know, but I fear they came to a sad end. Jamie did not inherit his mother's aversion to spiders, and the uncertainty attending the fate of the "little dears" his curiosity had turned out into the cold, caused the heart of the infant naturalist much concern.

PROSPECTING, AND WHAT I FOUND
IN MY DIGGING

ᘓᘏ

"All that glisters is not gold."
—*Merchant of Venice*[1]

ONE day last summer I was digging in the grove outside my garden for some fine black mould with which to pot some geraniums. While poking about with my spade at the roots of a decayed old stump, and stirring the surface of the loose earth and leaves, a glittering object caught my eye.

It was so bright that I really began to fancy that I had hit upon a treasure, perhaps a nugget, but when I continued to prospect for my gold, to my surprise it began to move, and presently a jet black creature, with coat like grained leather, decked with bright golden stars, came slowly struggling into view.

It was evidently of the lizard family, but unlike any specimen I had ever before met with. It was not a true lizard, as I found out later.

In length, from nose to the end of the tail, it was about ten inches. The back was marked with nine gold stars; there were also three on either side, three on each leg, one on each foot, and one on the head, which was flattish, and one on the nose,—altogether a very handsome set of ornaments shining with yellow lustre on its jet black coat.

Knowing the inoffensive nature of the creature, and that it would neither bite nor sting, I transferred it to my flower pot and carried it home that I might study it more at my leisure.

I have before alluded to my dislike for spiders and reptiles of all kinds, arising from an aversion to anything ugly or disgusting, and although this little creature was more remarkable for its handsome appearance than any of its kind, I still preferred looking at it to touching it, and was surprised at a young lady friend not only taking my lizard in her hand, but actually petting and patting it without the least reluctance or aversion.

My friend was, I found, quite a naturalist. She told me that she had seen a specimen of the same in Nova Scotia, where the species, though rare, was well known. She thought it belonged to a division of the Bactrian order, and that there were some eighty species native to North America, and many southward; possibly it belonged to the genus *Salamandria maculata*, or Spotted Salamander family.

After we had studied it to our hearts' content, and admired and counted its spots, it was consigned to a glass preserve jar half filled with water, and left in peace. Our prisoner did not, however, appear to be enjoying the bath as much as we expected he would, but on the contrary was evidently desirous of escaping the liquid element, raising his head and forefeet above the surface and looking anxiously through the transparent wall of his prison with rather a doleful expression of countenance.

He certainly was not happy, and I, having some compassion for poor "Gold Star" in his captive state, determined to release him. After a confinement of two days I opened the jar and took him back to his home under the stump in the grove. The released animal walked off very leisurely, but no doubt enjoyed the sense of liberty, which may be as dear to a salamander as to man.

Some time afterwards I was describing my capture to a gentleman who was much interested in the natural history of Ontario. He said it was a true salamander, belonging to the order *Urodela*, family *Salamandriæ*; that he had often seen both the spotted and gold-starred species in the forests of southern France, where they abound. Like all the tribe they are great insect devourers, and having no evil propensities are never destroyed by the country people.

When on the Continent, Mr. E_____ was a great frequenter of the woods, seeking for specimens of birds and insects, and would often stay his steps to watch and admire the beauty of the glittering coats and the lively movements of these little creatures as they darted to and fro or basked in the sunshine.

They are great lovers of heat, and it is from this no doubt the idea arose that the salamander could live unhurt by fire. This was a mistake of the ancients, or it may have been simply an exaggeration in alluding to the habits of the sun-loving animal.

Mr. E_____ thought this species was rare in eastern Canada, but might be found farther westward.

THE ROBIN AND THE MIRROR

YESTERDAY I noticed from my window a pair of robins paying many visits to a maple tree at the edge of the lawn. Much time was spent in flitting to and from, but there seemed to be no settled plan between the pair whether to build in the upper or lower branches, and no foundation was laid.

Today the male bird made his appearance without his mate, and he seemed restless and uneasy.

Now it happened that an accident had broken the glass in front of the Wardian[1] case appropriated to my ferns, and the servant had lifted it on the grass plot for a new light to be put in. The back of the case had been fitted with a plate of looking-glass, and as Master Robin flitted past he saw his own image in the glass and instantly flew to it, evidently with joy, thinking he recognized his absent and, I fear, faithless mate. Ruffling his feathers, spreading his wings, and pecking at the glass as if to invite her in the most loving manner to his breast, but finding his entreaties fruitless, he flew up to the maple—I suppose with the hope that the wife would respond to his call note and follow. Then down again the poor fellow came to renew his vain entreaties. More than half an hour was thus spent in and out of the case, up and down from the tree.

At last, having made a final dash at the glass, he went off in a fit of rage or astonishment at the behaviour of his most obdurate spouse. Like some men and women, Rob had taken the semblance for reality and been deceived.

A more touching and somewhat similar incident was one I witnessed when travelling in the country some years ago.

In the room into which I was shown by the mistress of the hotel was a large mirror, and while standing before it I noticed the strange behaviour of a pretty canary bird, which hovered with an impatient fluttering motion over my head; but on my moving away the little bird flew to the glass uttering a peculiar cry, and then a thrilling song was followed by the creature flying to the empty cage and back again to where its own pretty image was reflected in the glass, and which it evidently took for its mate.

On my remarking upon the strange actions of the canary, the mistress of the house told me that its mate had died, and that the poor widowed bird had never ceased its mourning. She had let it out of the cage because it was so unhappy, and seeing its own image had taken it for the dead mate.

"Indeed, madam," she said, "the creature is for all the world like us in its grief; it makes my own heart sad to see it take on so. I do not know what to do, for I love the little thing and fear it will destroy itself beating its breast on the glass.

I advised her to put it in the cage and cover it over so as to darken it awhile, or to take it out of the room where the mirror was, which I think she did.

In neither of these cases can we well refer the actions of the birds to the law of instinct alone.

IN THE CANADIAN WOODS

SPRING

"If thou art worn and hard beset
  With sorrows that thou wouldst forget,
  If thou wouldst read a lesson that will keep
  Thy heart from fainting and thy soul from sleep,
    Go to the woods and hills!—no tears
    Dim the sweet look that Nature wears."
                                    —*Longfellow*[1]

At no season of the year are the woods more attractive than in the early spring, when, weary of their snowy covering, we hail with increasing satisfaction the breaking forth of the tender leafage as it bursts from the brown buds which had encased it during the long months of frost and winter snows.

No newly hatched butterfly expanding its crumpled wings to the glad sunshine is more alive to the genial influence of sun and breeze than are the young opening leaves of the maple, poplar, beech and birch, as they greet the soft winds of April and May, and flutter forth into full free life. The very bark on the twigs takes a living freshness of tint and color, in place of the dull hard deadness of its winter hue.

In April the sap rises in the dark thready foliage of the pines, and the heavy boughs of the hemlock and spruce, those faithful hardy evergreens of the forest, brightening the sombre growth of former seasons with a rich tender verdure, harbinger of the brighter tints of later trees.

Then the American larch—the tamarac of the Indians—begins to put forth her light green leaves and hang out her rosy tassels of red buds all along the slender pendent branches. Beautiful as flowers are these soft red cones peeping out from the clusters of delicate thready leaves which guard them, and forming delightful contrasts to the deeper shades of the surrounding foliage.

It is the tough, elastic roots of the tamarac that are chiefly used by the Indians in making their birch-bark canoes. This is the "*wah-tap*," which, after it has been stripped from the yellow bark, and steeped for many hours in water to render it more supple, is coiled away ready for use.

The graceful tassels, or "catkins," as they are commonly called, of the willow and the birch, which have been growing in secret all through last autumn, are among the first buds of the hardwood forest trees to unfold, and are now "dancing in breezy mirth"[2] on every little spray. The least breath of wind sets them in motion, tossing them to and fro as though the whole tree were quivering with the joy of its new life.

Near by, but with less lively aspect, the stately elm shows its olive-tinted, furry flower buds in soft contrast to the pointed, shining red cases that enclose the foliage and fruitage of its neighbor, the graceful beech.

The first of all to give the tender color of spring to the distant woods are the quivering aspen and the silvery poplar. The trees on the outer edge of the forest, and within readier reach of the sun's rays, drink in their warmth and are the first to send out responsive life in opening bud and leaf, an earnest of all that is to follow when the fresh verdure shall clothe every bush and tree with its robe of life and beauty.

Then as the snow melts, the first forest flowers appear, the earliest to greet us being the Liver-leaf, or "Snow Flower," as the old settlers have appropriately named the *Hepatica triloba*. The sweetest of our spring flowers, it takes the place to us of the dear English primrose. The starry blossoms are pure white, and blue, and pink of several tints. They spring up all wrapped in silken sheen from the sheltering beds of the old leaves that have clung to them, as if to guard the hidden life from the bitter frosts of the lingering winter.

Then comes Spring Beauty, the *Claytonia Virginica,*

"That delicate forest flower,
With scented breath, and look so like a smile,
Seems, as it issues from the shapeless mould,
An emanation of the indwelling Life."
—*Bryant*[3]

Oro (Ontario), *1873,* by George Harlow White.

Hosts of violets of all shades follow, and are among the earliest of the forest flowers; but, alas, the ruthless advance of man upon the scene, in cutting down the sheltering trees, has robbed the spring flowers of the warm winter cloak which protected them from the bitter winds, so that while formerly we looked for these lovely flowers in April, we now seldom find them before May. Some indeed of the forest plants have disappeared and we see them no more. Types are they of the native race, the Indian children of the land, fast passing away.[4] "Thou shalt seek them in the morning, and shalt not find them."[5]

SUMMER

"Under the greenwood tree
 Who loves to lie with me,
 And turn his merry note
 Unto the sweet bird's throat,
Come hither, come hither, come hither:
 Here shall he see
 No enemy
But winter and rough weather."
                        —*As You Like It.*[6]

But it is no rough weather that we shall meet this lovely summer day if my reader will go with me into the forest glades.

Here is a pathway under the maples and beeches; let us follow it and see the woods in all their rich summer array. The June rains and July heat have deepened and strengthened their coloring and given matured life and vigor to leaf and branch, so that we shall find a richer though perhaps more subdued beauty of form and color than that of the tender loveliness of the spring.

Overhead the light semi-transparent leaves are all astir, quivering in the breeze as the sunshine comes fitfully down through the treetops and casts moving shadows on the dark mould below.

Looking around us we mark the endless variety of graceful forms in tree and leaf and flower. The earth is teeming with luxuriance, and one might almost fancy her conscious of all the wealth of vegetable treasures she bears on her capacious breast, and which she has brought forth and nourished.

Besides the lofty maples, oaks, beeches, elms and birches, there is the leafy basswood (American lime), scenting the air with the fragrance of its creamy blossoms, and, farther on, the subtle almond-like scent of the black cherry betrays its presence among the trees; though but for its scent we should not have distinguished it from among its loftier compeers of the wood.

Is it the gummy odor of the sweet birch that is so pleasant or is it the sweet scent of those lovely pyrolas that some of the country folks misname "lilies of the valley," but which the more learned botanist classes with the

Heath family, although the affinity to the heather is not apparent to the unlearned lover of wild flowers of the forest.

Among the less important forest trees, the bloom of the hornbeam attracts the eye, and truly no flower can hang more gracefully from its pendent spray than do these pretty greenish white sacs, resembling strongly the hop which one sees twining its tendrils about the lattice of many a poor settler's veranda in the backwoods, where it is cultivated alike for ornament and use.

The rough furry cases of the beechnuts are now giving an olive hue to the branches, and a darker, more sombre color to the light green foliage which so charmed us in the first flush of spring. There is on their laden branches the promise of an abundant supply for many of God's pensioners,[7] the squirrel, the field mouse, the groundhog, the porcupine, and others of the roving denizens of the woods and wilds. These creatures know well the time of the dropping of the glossy three-sided nuts, and hasten diligently to gather up their stores. They gather that they did not toil for or sow,[8] but their bountiful Father openeth His hand and filleth all things living with plenteousness.

How deep is the silence of the forest! A strange sweet sense of restful stillness seems to come down upon the soul. One scarcely cares to tread too roughly, for it is as if the shadow of the mighty God of all creation were around us calling for an unspoken prayer of praise and adoration.

We stand beneath the pines and enter the grand pillared aisles with a feeling of mute reverence; these stately trunks bearing their plumed heads so high above us seem a meet roofing for His temple who reared them to His praise. "Where is the house that ye build unto me?...Hath not my hand made all these things?"[9]

And hark! through the aerial harp strings, swept by the sighing winds, are there not hymns of melody and praise unheard by human ears that ascend up on high even to His throne? "O ye winds of God, praise Him and magnify His name forever!"[10]

There are melodies in ocean, earth and air, unheeded by man as he goes forth to his daily labor, but heard by unseen spirits in their ministrations of love fulfilling the will of our Father.[11]

Not many living creatures cross our path in these leafy solitudes, unless by chance we disturb some red squirrel from his seat on a moss-covered

fallen trunk. At our approach he darts up the nearest tree in swift gyra-
tions, for these little creatures climb in circles, first on one side then on
the other. The eye can scarcely follow his track until he reaches a projecting fork where he finds a hiding place; there, made bolder by distance,
he stops to look down, perhaps not in fear but with curiosity and something of displeasure, upon the unwelcome intruder. He expresses his
anger by uttering sharp scolding notes, setting up his fine furry tail as a
banner of defiance.

Listen to that soft whispering sound. It cannot be called a song, it is so
soft and monotonous. It is the note of a tiny brown bird that flits among
the pine cones, one of the little treecreepers, a Sitta or a Certhia, gentle
birds small as the tiniest of our wrens.

They live among the cone-bearing evergreens, gleaning their daily meal
from between the chinks of the rugged bark where they find the larvae
upon which they feed.

As they flit to and fro they utter this little call-note to their companions, so soft that it would pass unnoticed but for the silence that reigns
around us.

We call this little denizen of the pine forest the "Whisperer," and I have
some doubt if I am right in supposing it to be a Certhia or a Sitta. I cannot recognize it in Mr. McIlwraith's "Birds of Ontario." I know it only as
a tiny brown treecreeper, that runs up and down the trees uttering its soft
whispering note. It is smaller and less pretty than the tiny black and white
spotted woodpecker that comes to the trees in my garden or taps with its
strong bill on the shingled roof of the house—a quick, noisy rapping, as
much as to say, "Here I am!—here I am!" Or perhaps I see a pair of these
pretty fellows busy on the moss-crusted garden fence. So busy are they
that they will let one come within a few feet of them before they dart off
to the nearest tree or post. One kind is striped, with a red spot on its head;
the larger ones are more spotted.

Though there is less luxuriance in the herbage growing beneath the
pines than under the maples and beeches, we yet find some rare and lovely plants flourishing there that are not found in the richer soil under the
hardwood trees.

Many of the little evergreens known by the familiar and descriptive name
of wintergreens abound, especially the beautiful starry-flowered pyrolas.

Here is one, the *Pipsissewa* or "Rheumatism Weed" of the herbalist, with the glossy shining leaves and lovely wax-like pink flowers. It is a floral gem. Mark its rosy stem, its dark green serrated leaves and umbel of pink-tinted flowers. Within the hollow of each petal we see the stamens and amethyst-colored anthers surrounding the thick-ribbed, turban-shaped stigma in the centre of emerald green. Who can look upon this exquisite flower without a feeling of pleasure? It seems to me perfect in all its parts.

There are many others of this family growing in the woods, but they generally prefer the richer soil under the hardwood trees, where also they can get more moisture.

Of these the *Moneses uniflora* is one of the most beautiful. It has but one pure milk-white blossom, each petal elegantly scalloped, and sending forth a delicious perfume. The pistil of the *Moneses* is most singular. It is much longer than the closely appressed stamens, and terminates in a little bright green pointed crown somewhat inclining downward. This plant is rare.

There is another small species less fragrant, the flower of which is greenish white and inferior in beauty to the milk white and larger plants.

Where the ground inclines to be rocky, or in the vicinity of water, we come upon a bed of sweet May flower. It is rather late this year. May and June are its months for blooming, but some will linger in shady damp spots, even on into July and August.

> "Sweet flowers that linger ere they fade,
>   Whose last are sweetest."[12]

What a gummy fragrance about this charming plant with the pink bells, red stems and oval leaves! It is in the mossy glands of the stalks and buds that the aroma lies and is given out from this beautiful Creeping Arbutus, for it belongs to that charming ornamental family. It would be a desirable addition to the trailing plants of our rockeries and hanging baskets could we prevail upon it to abide with us, but it loves too well its own wild rocky forest haunts, and the piny soil its rootlets find in the crevices between the stones, to readily change its habits.

Creeping over little hillocks in shady ground we see that kindly little evergreen, the dark round-leafed Partridge Berry (*Mitchella repens*), with its fragrant starry white blossoms, and at the foot of that old hemlock spruce there is a cluster of orchids, the handsome striped or coral-rooted orchids.

These showy flowers come up destitute of green leaves, but with many stems, some more than a foot in height and loaded with flowers of a pale fawn color, striped with deep crimson. Silvery scales take the place of leaf and bract, and there are often from ten to twenty or thirty flowers on the scaly stems, a mass of fine color growing closely together. The irregular white-knobbed root stalk has given it the name of Coral Root (*Corallorhiza multiflora*).

There are other species of the orchid family dispersed among the pines, though it is generally in boggy or peaty soil these rare and singular plants are found. Yet here is a near connection—and one often found in the pine woods, where we notice it growing on the decaying trunk of some fallen tree—the pearly-flowered Rattlesnake Plantain (*Goodyera repens*). Its deep green leaves, with the milk-white traceries over their surface and the semi-transparent sac-lipped little flower, surely make it deserving of a better name, and one more in keeping with its near neighbor and relative, the Ladies' Tresses, so-called from the spiral arrangement of its leaves and stalks.

But the slanting sunbeams gilding the red trunks of the pines warn me it is time to retrace my steps, and the sound of the jangling cowbells speaks audibly of the hour when the children will be looking for their tea.

AUTUMN

"See how the great old forest vies
  With all the glories of the skies,
    In streaks without a name;
  And leagues on leagues of scarlet spires,
  And temples lit with crimson fires,
    And palaces of flame!
  And domes on domes that gleam afar,
  Through many a gold and crimson bar
    With azure overhead;
  While forts, with towers on towers arise,
  As if they meant to scale the skies,
    With banners bloody red."
                    —*Alexander McLachlan*[13]

Silently but surely the summer with all its wealth of flower has left us, though we still have a few of its latest blossoms lingering on into the ripened glory of the autumn days. Our roadsides and waste places are brilliant with the gay waving Goldenrod (*Solidago*)—that sun-loving flower which does not fade and droop its golden spikes under the August and September heat.

Graceful asters, too, of many sorts are blooming in sunshine and in shade, and many a beautiful gentian, both the fringed-flower of the poet and the later variety, have I gathered late in October.

August suns have ripened the grain, and the harvest moon has set over the fields now ready for the plough, where the sower will soon be abroad scattering the seed for another year.

God's silent workers have not been idle. They have gathered in the harvest on plain and wayside wastes, on lonely lake shore and by the banks of the gliding river. The dormouse and the ground squirrel (our little striped chipmunk), and the red and black squirrel have already begun to lay by stores of kernels, seeds and grain. The musquash, the otter and the beaver may delay yet a little till the frosty nights warn them that "time and tide wait for no man,"[14] nor yet for the wild creatures that build by forest, lake and stream.

The brown acorns, glossy and shining, now fall with every wind that shakes the branches. The rugged husks of the beech have opened wide to let the bright three-sided mast fall to the earth to be gathered up by "the wild flock that never need a fold."[15]

Truly, it is wonderfully strange, yet true, that each one knows exactly how much it will require to keep its family during the winter months. Here is a calculation that defies many a thrifty human housekeeper. He that gathers much hath nothing over, and he that gathers little hath no lack.[16]

The pines are strewing the ground with a soft carpet of spiny needle-like leaves, the product of former seasons, and already, early in September, a few brilliant scarlet leaves have appeared among the green of the maples, while the birch and poplar hang out their golden banners, soon to scatter them abroad. Not less attractive are the young beeches as seen against the full dark green of the spruce and hemlock.

On the outskirts of the wood, or on the bank of lake or stream, the eye is caught by fringes of every hue, the red of the osier beds, the high bush cranberry with its purplish tinge of foliage and rich crimson fruit, while the glorious scarlet of the prinos, or "winter berry," like the holly of the motherland, charms us by its gay fruitage. The old settlers call this fine shrub—for it does not attain to the dignity of a tree—the "Pigeon Berry."

I know a rocky island in Stony Lake, not far from our own little island of Minnewawa, where there is a splendid bush laden with the berries and dark shining leaves; a lovely object it appeared reflected on the still bosom of the lake that bright September morning. What a feast for the wild birds! One almost envied them their treat.

The juniper and the red cedar, too, are very beautiful; the mealy whiteness of the one and the blue tints of the clustering berries of the other are now in perfection, ready for the little hoarders of the fruits of the wilderness.

Of all the seasons in Canada, that of September is the most enjoyable. Heat we have for a short time, but not overpowering. The summer indeed is gone, but there is a dreamy softness, a fulness and finish, if I may so express it, that is very near perfection. This is the pause before the equinoctial gales come to rend the trees and strew the earth with a rich covering of leaves, ere the Frost King[17] has with his nipping fingers touched the oak, the maple, the elm and the beech, changing their green leaves to every shade of crimson, scarlet, orange, yellow, and russet brown. These colors, as the days steal by, light up the landscape with a passing glory— a glory that has with it a sense of sadness, too, for it is the beauty that heralds in decay—Nature's fever glow on the cheek of the dying year.

An English artist, accustomed to study the more sober hues of the foliage in the woods and hedgerows of his own country, gazed with almost despairing eyes upon one of our glowing autumnal landscapes. Striking his hands together, he exclaimed: "Those contrasts of color are too brilliant! Those cloudless skies, that deep blue water, those gorgeous scarlets, orange and reds—how can such a scene as this be rendered faithfully as a truthful picture of Canadian scenery? 'What exaggeration!' would be the verdict. How can I tone it all down to be believed in? Yet how surpassingly beautiful it is!"

But the lovely pageantry soon disappears. A day of pouring rain, a sweeping wind or night of frost, and the glory has departed, and we may write upon it, "Ichabod,"[18] while the breeze sounds its requiem in wails and sobs among the leafless boughs, or shivers with rustling sound the leaves still clinging to the young beeches and oak saplings in the forest.

There is a change in the climate since the time when we used to look for the Indian summer. The destruction of the forest trees has told upon it in many ways. We feel it in the sweep of the wind in autumn and spring especially, in the drifting snow of winter, and in the growing scarcity of the fish in our lakes.

Those soft calm days of November or late October are now seldom experienced—the frosty nights, misty mornings, and warm days when the sun, veiled by the smoky atmosphere, looked red and strange, yet not inspiring fear—day after day of changeless calm which the natives call Indian summer, claiming it as if it of right belonged to them. "Our summer," they say; "the month of our harvest of rice, the hunter's month, the fisher's month"—thus they call the last three months of the year. But with the forests the Indians and their summer are both passing away.

My sister's lines on the Indian Summer may well be quoted here:

"By the purple haze that lies
    On the distant rocky height,
By the deep blue of the skies,
    By the smoky amber light
Through the forest arches streaming,
Where Nature on her throne sits dreaming,
And the sun is scarcely gleaming
    Through the cloudlets, snowy white,—
Winter's lovely herald greets us
Ere the ice-crowned tyrant meets us.

"This dreary Indian summer day
    Attunes the soul to tender sadness;
We love—but not joy in the ray;
    It is not summer's fervid gladness,
But a melancholy glory
    Hovering softly round decay,—
Like swan that sings her own sad story
    Ere she floats in death away."
                    —*Susanna Moodie*[19]

WINTER

"Sharp is the frost, the Northern Light
  Flickers and shoots its streamers bright;
  Snowdrifts cumber the untracked road,
  Bends the pine with its heavy load."
                    —*Francis Rye*[20]

There is silence in the forest. The birds that came to make their summer sojourn here have long since forsaken us. All are gone—not a song, not a twitter or chirp, meets the ear. Even the lively little ground squirrel has gathered in his stores and retired to his warm, cosy house under the root of oak or beech, where, within reach of his well-filled granary, he is snugly cuddled with his furry family, a happy denizen of his native woods. The bolder, hardier red squirrel is safely housed in the fork of a hollow tree, sheltered from blustering winds and drifting snow. The racoon, the porcupine, the little field mouse, are all hidden in nest or burrow, and even the bears with their cubs are sleeping in their secret haunts.

Few indeed of the hardier birds that winter with us are now seen to venture from the close coverts of the dense cedar swamps; only on chance sunny days the crossbill, the pine grosbeak or the hardy blue jay will come near our dwellings, and the little spotted woodpecker will be heard upon the trunk of some neighboring monarch of the forest tapping and rapping as busy as a bee.

The hunter and the lumberman may sometimes catch sight of the little treecreeper and the titmouse flitting among the pines in search of the insects hidden in the bark and cones, or hear the rapid sonorous strokes of the large woodpecker,—the red-capped "cock of the woods"—hammering away on some old tree and stripping down great sheets of bark from the fast decaying trunk; but only in the thickest of the forest would this be, for rarely is this large species met with elsewhere.

The ruffed grouse that is commonly called "wood partridge" is not migratory; both it and the spruce partridge abide the winter hidden in the spruce and hemlock woods. All through the cold months of the Canadian season they feed on the scanty berries of the wintergreen, the buds of spruce, and the red bark of the wild raspberry. The latter imparts a red tinge and much bitterness to the flesh, and by the month of February renders it unfit for food.

The Frost King is abroad, and as by the magic touch of an enchanter's wand has wrought a wondrous change within the forest as well as on lake and stream.[21]

What has become of the unsightly heaps of brushwood, the *débris* of fallen rotting leaves, of stalks of withered flowers and rank herbage, the blackened stumps, the old prostrate wind-blown trees? Where are they now? Here is purity without a sign of decay. All that offended the sight in our forest walks has vanished.

A spotless robe of dazzling whiteness, soft and bright as the swan's downy breast, is spread over all that was unsightly. The new-fallen snow decks every fan-like spray of hemlock, balsam fir, and spruce, with mimic wreaths of fairy flowers. The young saplings, weak and slender, bend beneath their burden, lightly as it seems to lie upon them, weighing them down until they touch the ground, forming bowers and graceful arcades of crystal brightness; even the very stumps are dressed with turbans whiter than the far-famed looms of Decca[22] could weave or art of fuller whiten.

A Pine Stump in Canada, Oro (Ontario), *22 January 1873,* by George Harlow White.

Looking upward we see a hazy veil above the dark funereal pine tops, through which the silvery stars gleam softly, while fantastic shadows checker the glittering snow beneath our feet. All about us is a stillness so profound that it would seem as if Nature herself lay wrapped in sleep.

The dull creaking of our footsteps on the closely packed snow, the fall of a dry pine cone, or the cracking of the frost-bound bark of some distant forest tree, alone breaks the silence. Is there no sound or sight of living thing? Yes; see those tiny marks upon the surface of the snow—footprints so small that but for the long line reaching from tree to tree they would escape the quickest sight. Some living thing has been here. It is the tiniest of all quadrupeds, the little "jumping mouse," or zerboa. A brave little animal, fearless of cold and frozen snow, it has ventured from its domicile in search of food. It would not come out just for play in the cold moonlight. One cannot suspect the fairy creature of any such motive; but motive it must have, and it keeps it to itself. Well is it if no midnight owl or the white arctic hawk which is sometimes seen in the dense forest does not pounce upon its defenceless head and bear it off as a prize. I have seen these pretty little mice in the summer, and admired their agile, skipping ways; but in the winter, though seeing many a track of their fairy feet on the snow, I have never observed the little creatures themselves.

In an old diary I have notes, written years ago, of sleigh drives in a rude vehicle, when, wrapped in buffalo and bear skins, lying at ease with my little ones cuddled up from the keen wintry cold, we made many a moonlight visit to some friend. What a merry, noisy party we were, singing and laughing and chattering as we sped through the snow-laden forest road— a rough road and a wild one it was then, more than fifty years ago.

What changes the years have brought! Where now are the pine woods? Where the log house, the primeval settlement house; the disfiguring stump in the newly-cleared fallows; the ugly snake-like rail fences, the rude enclosures of the first efforts of the immigrant; the jangling sound of the cattle bells, the lumber sleighs? All are gone—things that *were*, not things that *are*.

Fair dwellings, tasteful gardens, fruitful orchards, the village schoolhouse, the church spire, the busy factory, the iron-girdered bridge, the steamboat, the railroad, the telegraph, the telephone—these have taken the place of the lonely forest settlements.

"Old things are passed away: behold, all things are become new."[23] Slowly and surely the march of civilization has gone on, yet "seed time and harvest, summer and winter"[24] have returned according to their circuits; and as I look back through the long vista of the past I can trace the guiding hand of Him who changeth not.[25]

A SONG FOR A SLEIGH DRIVE

Tune: "Farewell to Glen Owen"—*Welsh air*

Hurrah for the forest! the dark pine wood forest!
The sleigh bells are jingling with musical chimes;
 The woods still are ringing
 As gayly we're singing —
Oh, merry it is in the cold winter time.

Hurrah for the forest! the dark pine wood forest!
With the moon stealing down on the cold frozen snow.
 With eyes beaming brightly,
 And hearts beating lightly,
Through the wild forest by moonlight we go.

Hurrah for the forest! the dim ancient forest!
Where silence and stillness for ages have been.
 We'll rouse the grim bear,
 And the wolf from his lair,
And the deer shall start up from the thick cedar screen.

Oh, wail for the forest! the green shady forest!
No longer its depths may the hunter explore;
 For the bright golden grain
 Shall wave o'er the plain.
Oh, wail for the forest, its glories are o'er![26]

THE FIRST DEATH IN THE CLEARING*[1]

⁓

"There is no flock, however watched and tended,
But one dead lamb is there!
There is no fireside, howsoe'er defended,
But has one vacant chair."

—Longfellow[2]

ONE lovely morning, early in April, I was standing at the window that overlooked the lake and its dark-fringed shore, watching the wildfowl that were gathered in flocks about the pools of blue water where the warm sunshine had melted the ice. My little boy was in my arms evidently enjoying the lively movements of the birds as they dashed and splashed the water over themselves. There were wild geese, ducks and herons, and above them hovered a big baldheaded eagle ready to swoop down upon any luckless fowl that he might mark for his prey.

I was so interested in the scene that I did not hear the step of a barefooted child behind me until a little figure, wrapped in a faded tartan shawl, laid her hand upon my arm and in a strong Scotch accent said:

"Mistress, ye maun come awa' the noo wi' me to see the wee ane. The mither is aye greeting and sent me ower to bid ye come to see till't."

"And who is it that sent you?" I asked.

*From my Journal, April 6th, 1834.

"The mither o' the sick wean, Mrs. P___, at the Falls."

"But," I said, "my little maid, what can I do for the sick child?"

"I dinna ken, but ye maun come."

Though from Maggie's further description of the state of the babe I feared I could do little for the sufferer, I thought I might do somewhat to comfort the poor young mother, so I put on my plaid and hood and followed my little guide.

"She stayed not for brake and stopped not for stone,"[3] but led the way fearlessly over the most impracticable-looking places, sometimes climbing over log heaps, dashing through puddles of melting snow, creeping along fallen, half-rotted logs beside pools where even the little will-o'-the-wisp was not sure of a safe passage, and often stretching out a strong red fist to aid me when I faltered on the way.

At last the house was reached without accident, and I found the young mother sorrowfully regarding the sick infant. It was lying in a rude cradle, pale as death, wasted almost to a shadow, and exhausted from its last fit of convulsions. I had seen it in her arms only a week before a picture of infantile health and beauty, for indeed it was a lovely babe. Though so young, its pretty head was thick with curls; now lax and damp they hung round the brow on which death had already set its seal. Poor Jessie! poor mother!

"It cannot live," she said mournfully, looking up in my face as if to ask for some word to give her a ray of hope. Alas! she saw I could give her none. The Lord of life alone could restore that fading flower, for "Life's young wings were fluttering for their flight."[4]

We put the baby into a warm bath to try and stay the attacks, but in vain; every half hour fresh fits convulsed the tender frame, each one threatening to be the last effort of expiring life.

It was saddening to see the intense anguish of the mother as she stopped from the work she was compelled to attend to (cooking for the mill hands) to bend over her dying babe, suppressing the grief that none but a mother can feel. I could help her only by holding the child in my lap or watching beside it.

Jessie's husband was the overseer of the busy workmen employed at the buildings then being erected at the mills, and the wife had to cook for all the men. The master was young and had little sympathy for the poor young mother. What was a babe of the overseer's to him! The ready meals for the men must not be neglected, and she must attend to and fulfil her covenanted duties, babe or no babe. His hard heart was not softened by the sight of the poor mother's yearning, tearful eyes as she turned them so sadly on her dying child; but some of the more sympathetic among the men tried to cheer her by saying the child might yet recover, and though they knew the hope was not to be realized, it was kindly spoken.

Interior of a Settler's Shanty. Near Huntsville, August, 1871, by George Harlow White.

As night drew on I knew the child must die, and as I had not the heart to leave the poor mother alone with her great sorrow, I despatched a messenger to my own house to say I should not be home till morning. I prevailed on Jessie to lie down on her bed while I kept vigil, and glad I was to see the weary heart at rest after the day of toil and grief.

The infant slept, too, its last sleep on earth, to waken to a new life in heaven.

The first grey streaks of morning light found me still a watcher. The frosty air blew bleak and chill through the chinks in the imperfect wooden walls of the barrack-like building. Carefully replacing my sleeping charge in the cradle, I opened the door and went forth to look upon the face of the earth and the heavens, for my eyes were weary and my heart was sad.

Truly a lovely sight it was that met my view. The frosted ground was gemmed with countless mimic stars, glittering beneath as brightly as the stars in the blue sky above were gleaming ere they paled before the saffron light of the dawning day now streaking the eastern horizon. The mist was rising in clouds from the river where the rapids were tossing their white-crested heads beneath the shadows of the pines that clothed the opposite shores, grand and beautiful, untouched by the hand of man. What a contrast to the confusion spread around the recently erected mill and the half-finished, unsightly buildings, where heaps of refuse, piles of chips and bark strewed the ground!

No one was awake or stirring—not a sound was heard save the wild rushing sweep of the restless river as it dashed over its rocky bed, unchecked in its downward course by mill dams or sawlogs, its clear waters unpolluted by sawdust or bark, nor ploughed and stirred by steamboats and the rafts and cribs of the lumbermen.

I turned once more to the contemplation of human suffering. Without all was joy and life; within was sorrow and death.

I found Jessie awake and watching by the cradle of her little one, her hopes risen with the new day. The babe lay still and sleeping, and she thought it might yet recover. Knowing that I was needed at home by my own little one, and leaving Jessie with a promise to return, I set out on my solitary walk.

The day was now fairly opened. The ground was hard and crisp, and though keen, the fresh air of the early morning refreshed and revived me.

Nature herself had as it were been enjoying perfect rest, and with the sun had awakened to a newness of life.[5] The living creatures were lifting up their voices in hymns of praise and thanksgiving to Him from whom all blessings flow,[6] whose goodness had protected them through the night, and whose bounty was still to preserve them through the coming day.

There were songs and twitterings from birds rarely heard in the full glare of day. The red squirrels were out and abroad, crossing my path, while the little chipmunk stopped and set up his furry tail and chattered as if he would inquire what business I had out among his haunts at that early hour in the morning.

The robins had just arrived in the clearing, and it was a treat to hear the full song they poured forth. The rapping of the woodpecker and sharp shrill note of the blue jay jarred on my ear as I listened for the soft whispering of the little brown certhia or the livelier trill of the wren.

All these sweet sounds came with a soothing influence to my spirit, and in after years the memories of them come back to the mind wearied with the toil and moil of life, like the psalms and hymns we learned as children, to refresh us and lead us back from earth to heaven.

That evening I went back to the Falls to find the poor mother overwhelmed with grief. The child had died in that last sleep. It was her first-born treasure, and her grief was sore. I did my best to comfort her, although I had not then known the pang of a bereaved mother's heart. God gave me that trial in after years. I could only mingle my tears with hers, and even that human sympathy was something to the grieving heart. Once she looked down upon her arm and cried, "It used to lie here, and I shall never feel it here sae near to my ain heart again."

Jessie never forgot that babe; it lay very near to her warm motherly heart long after it had been forgotten by everyone but her.

The next day was the Sabbath, and the child's funeral was to take place at noon. The door being open I entered the darkened room without knocking. I shall never forget the feeling of solemn awe that came over me as I crossed the threshold from the bright noonday sunshine into the hushed gloom of the house of mourning.

There was no funeral pomp or display, no outward demonstration. A table in the centre of the room was covered with a damask cloth of snowy whiteness; beside it sat the child's father, a grave respectable Scotchman, in black, his hat craped and tied with the white ribbon symbol of the youth and innocence of the dead babe. A large Bible lay before him. He just raised his head from the book as my shadow fell upon the page, and bowed reverently and in silence as I passed over to where the mother bent above the little coffin.

I see her now in her black dress, her fair hair, like a golden veil gemmed with tears, almost shrouding, the calm sweet face of her dead. There was no violence in the subdued grief of the mourner. She took a little packet from her breast, and opening its folds pointed to the bright silken curls that she had cut from the pretty head, then replaced it with a sigh in the bosom where the soft head had been so tenderly nestled. It was only when the bearers came in and closed the coffin lid that forever hid her darling from her sight that, with a burst of grief not to be suppressed, she threw herself into my arms and wailed the piteous cry, "Gone! gone! My wean! my wean!"

Then she besought me to join the little funeral procession to the burying ground across the river, but this I could not do, for the way was far and I did not feel equal to the long walk.

I watched them as they crossed the bridge and ascended the opposite bank, till the white pall was lost among the dark pines that marked the forest road, and then with heavy heart retraced my steps to my own home.

THE EARLY BLEST

(Lines by my sister, Agnes Strickland)

Thy mother's sad eyes in wild anguish wept o'er thee,
And the tears of a father flowed fast to deplore thee;
And thine own feeble cries told the struggle within,
When thou, sinless babe, paid the forfeit of sin.

There was speechless despair when life's last rose had faded,
And thy death-darkened eyes with their cold lids were shaded,
And thy young limbs were wrapped in the robes of the dead,
And forever consigned to their lone narrow bed.

They mourned for the hope that affection had cherished;
They saw it in dust, and they deemed it had perished;
But they knew not that mercy directed the blow
That laid their beloved and beautiful low.

Like the blossom that's plucked ere rude winds have profaned it,
Or the snow-wreath that melts ere the soil has disdained it,
Thou wert snatched from a world of corruption and strife,
And saved from the cares and temptations of life.

They heard not the summons, exultingly given,
Which called thee from earth and its conflicts to heaven;
They saw not the prospects which brightened around thee
When the cold hand of death in its fetters had bound thee:
They heard not the joy-notes triumphant and clear
Which angels exultingly poured on thy ear:

"Heir of mortal sin and pain,
  Thou has 'scaped each earthly stain.
  Child of sorrow, care, and woe,
  Grief and care thou ne'er wilt know;
  Life's dark page can never be,
  Happy babe, unrolled to thee;
  Tears can never dim that eye
  Brightening now with ecstasy!

"Child, whom Jesus died to save,
  Wake and triumph o'er the grave!
  Cast its gloomy thralls aside;
  Thou art freed and justified!
  Death hath touched, but could not slay -
  Heir of glory, come away!

"Leave the sable bier and shroud,
  Mount the morning's golden cloud;
  Come through realms of azure space!
  Come to thine appointed place!
  Thou wert purchased with a price;
  Thou shalt enter Paradise.

"Come through sunbright fields of air,
  Ever shining, ever fair;
  Come where blessed spirits dwell;
  Come to joys ineffable;
  Come through boundless fields of space;
  Come to thine appointed place.

"Come where heavenward souls are winging;
  Come where angel harps are ringing;
  Come where seraphs ever cry,
  'Glory be to God on high!'
  Come where shining cherubim
  Pour the everlasting hymn.
  Thou shalt join that radiant train;
  Thou wilt swell their raptured strain.

"Come, thou highly favored one!
 Come before thy Maker's throne;
 Come where guilt can never sever;
 Come and praise the Lord forever."[7]

ALONE IN THE FOREST[1]

THE first impetus that our neighborhood received was the putting up of a sawmill at the Falls of the Otonabee, about half a mile below my brother's house, and the building of a bridge to connect the townships of Douro and Smith, thus giving a better access to the town of Peterborough, then (1833) the only market for our produce and for the purchase of household necessaries.

The clack of the mill wheels was soon mingling with the sound of the rush of the rapids, and we were able to obtain the requisite lumber to complete the new log house, and subsequently to build a frame barn and stable for the cattle.

The proprietor of the mill was an adventurous young Scotchman, very ambitious and sanguine, but who illustrated the truth of the Italian proverb, "His beak is longer than his wings."[2]

He went home on speculation for a wife, and succeeded in persuading a young lady who had some money to accept him and return with him to Canada. Accustomed to the enjoyment of all the comforts which independent means enabled her to command in the Old World, it was little wonder that the young wife beheld with dismay the homeliness of her new surroundings in the backwoods.

She had felt the fatigue of a journey through the sombre pine forest, and turned with deep disgust from the unsightly prospect of half-cleared fields, disfigured by charred stumps and surrounded by scorched and blackened trees, in the midst of which lay her new home.

Where was the charming rural village her husband had spoken of with pride and delight? Here was only a sawmill—never a pleasant sight— heaps of newly sawn boards, all the *débris* of bark and chips, and the skeleton frames of unfinished buildings scattered without order over the rough ground. The stone house to which she was introduced as her future residence consisted simply of two rooms on the ground floor and two small bedrooms above, with a kitchen, a wide barrack-like lean-to built of boards against the main edifice.

Is it to be wondered that a feeling of disappointment and discontent took possession of her, and that, unable to see the future with her husband's sanguine, hopeful eyes, she should often weep and sigh over her lot; that she should feel the change from her former life, and that the remembrance of all she had lost in her own beloved country should make the contrast more painful?

Yet, though very miserable at times, she clung with passionate affection to her husband. With womanly devotion she made all sorts of excuses for him; she would not, could not, believe that he had willingly deceived her or had married her from interested motives. This love, as it grew stronger, upheld her in the sad reality of utter ruin, for truly misfortune like an armed force came soon upon them, and every fair and flattering prospect vanished. Unable to command the money to meet the claims of importunate creditors, or to satisfy the workmen clamoring at his door daily for their wages, her husband was obliged to give up under a sheriff's warrant all the property he possessed, and to find himself a prisoner in his own house. Only on Sundays was he free to go abroad. No entreaties availed to obtain any portion of the principal of his wife's property, and it was fortunate for them that it was so vested in the hands of trustees as to be beyond the reach of any claim from the creditors, as the interest on it alone kept the unfortunate debtors from starvation.

With these trials and privations came a courage and strength of mind to do and to bear. The young wife had no former experience of hardships, but when encountered she bore them bravely. She was now a mother, and the unwonted cares of maternity were added to other arduous duties. She often lamented over her want of knowledge in the management of her baby; she had never been accustomed to see young children otherwise than in the nursery of a friend under the care of nurses, and tending on an infant was an entirely new experience, which troubled her much.

To add to her labors ague attacked her husband, and to a young active man confinement to his bedroom or to the house was, no doubt, very trying. To do him justice, he was always kind and considerate to his wife, and when not suffering under the effects of the ague, took much of the care of the babe upon himself.

One by one my poor friend parted with her jewelry and her rich silks and satins, in order to raise the means of defraying the wages of a servant to perform such services as she was totally unused to and unfitted for. She was fond of flowers, but finding it useless to try and cultivate them in the rough stony ground about her house, she gave it up and was content with the few I could give her from my garden.

She came often to see me to ask advice about the baby, or for milk or other necessaries when in need of them. She knew that I took a kindly interest in her, and that she was always sure of sympathy and my husband's help if required in any difficulty. He pitied the misfortunes of her husband, and felt for them both in their trials.

A longer interval than usual having elapsed without a visit from my friend, and fearing that she, too, had fallen a victim to the ague, I walked over to ascertain the cause of her long absence. I found her lying on the rude couch which her ingenuity and resource had manufactured to supply the place of the furniture seized by the sheriff's officers. She looked very pale, and her beautiful fair hair hung all dishevelled about her neck and shoulders, as if she were too weary to gather it up.

I expressed my fear that she had taken the ague or lake fever, but she said, "No, it is only fatigue, not illness; for do you know, I was out wandering, lost for awhile in the woods last night."

"On what errand?" I asked in surprise, for I knew she rarely left the clearing.

"I had reason to expect letters from Scotland," she replied, "and I could trust no one about the place to go for them—indeed the business could only be done by myself—so leaving my boy with his father and the servant, I set off to walk to the town, with my good old dog Nelson for company and protection. I got my letters all right, made such purchases as were needed, and with my bundle was preparing to return—for the day was advancing to dusk—but Nelson was missing. I went to every place I had been to during the day without finding him, and, weary and anxious, I was obliged to turn my steps homeward alone.

"The moon was young, and I feared the light would fail me before I could make my way through the dark forest. You know what a cowardly dread I have of wolves and bears, and I do not love these lonely, gloomy woods.

Two Shanties on the Coldwater Road, Orillia Township, Ontario, September 1844, by Titus Hibbert Ware.

"I pushed on for the first hour as fast as I was able to walk. I was really tired, and my mind was harassed about leaving the dog behind me. I thought, too, of my sick husband and my boy, so that I did not dare to linger or stop to rest.

"My mind was so full of anxious thoughts that the way appeared more dreary; everything was so silent and death-like that my own footsteps startled me as they fell upon the fallen leaves; even the cracking of the dry sticks on the path wakened foolish nervous fears. So absorbed was I by these needless terrors that I did not notice at first that I had reached a point where two paths met and branched off in opposite directions, and I became sorely perplexed as to which was the right one to follow.

"After I had advanced for some time on the one I had chosen, my mind misgave me, and I hastily retraced my steps, not satisfied that I had taken the right path, and, unfortunately, decided upon following the other, which proved to be the wrong one. I hurried on, hoping to make up for the time I had lost by my indecision.

"The increasing gloom, deepened by a growth of hemlocks and cedars, made me think I was drawing near to the river and should soon find the bridge and the mill. Still, I could not recognize some of the pines that I had marked in my walk in the morning.

"My heart thrilled with terror as I heard the long-drawn howl of what I thought was a wolf in the cedar swamp that I had entered; the path, too, grew narrower and darker.

A First Settlement, by W.H. Bartlett, in Willis' *Canadian Scenery* (1848).

"My first impulse, when I heard that terrible sound, was to turn and flee for my life, but all my strength failed me at once, and I was compelled to sit down on the trunk of a fallen tree to recover myself. I remember crying out aloud. Alone, lost! lost in these dreadful woods, to perish by the fangs of wolves. What, what shall I do? Lord, save me, a poor lone wanderer! O my God, help me.[3] Such, dear friend, was my agonized prayer as I sat there in the dark forest.

"Then came the rapid sound of some animal rushing toward me at full speed, crashing the dry branches as it came. I felt that to escape was impossible, and started to my feet, while the wild beating of my heart was so loud that I heard no other sound.

"You may judge of the relief I experienced when my dear dog, my faithful Nelson, bounded towards me almost as panting and breathless as his terror-stricken mistress.

"You know I do not often indulge in tears, even when overwhelmed with trouble, but in this instance I fairly cried—but it was for joy—and I lifted up my heart in fervent thankfulness to Him who in His mercy and pity had guided my dumb protector through the tangled bush to my side that night. I could not help saying, 'Come, dear old Nelson, you have made a man of me! I shall fear neither wolf nor bear while I have you beside me.' Nelson was a powerful Newfoundland dog, and as brave as a lion.

"I fastened my bundle about his neck, and he trotted beside me, proud of the burden of which my arms had become very weary.

"I thought I would return and try the track I followed first, but noticing that there was a clearing of the trees ahead of me, I pushed on, thinking I was not far from some lumberer's shanty or the log house of one of the Irish settlers. Nor was I mistaken, for a few minutes brought me to the edge of a newly chopped fallow, and I heard the barking of a dog, which I had mistaken for the cry of a wolf.

"The moon had set, and I judged it must be getting late into the night. I peeped through the curtainless window of the shanty. The glimmering light from a few burning brands on the hearth and the smouldering red embers of a huge back log in the wide, clay-built chimney showed me the interior of the rude cabin.

"The inmates were all sleeping soundly. The growling of the cur as he retreated in fear of my big dog had failed to rouse them, so I took French leave[4] and stepped in without further ceremony than a light tap with my hand on the door.

"On a rude bed in the recess formed between the log walls and the chimney lay two women. One, the elder, not undressed, was lying on the coverlet, while the younger with fever-flushed cheeks lay restlessly tossing on the bed beside her.

"It was with some difficulty that I managed to rouse the elder woman to a consciousness of my presence and make her understand that I wanted a guide to the mill.

" 'Och! och! me dear craythure,' she exclaimed, as she raised herself on her brawny elbow and gazed at me from under a mass of tangled locks, a curious look in her black eyes: 'what for should a young thing like yerself be doin' up an' abroad at sich a time o' night. Shure an' it must be near the mornin'.'"

" 'My good woman,' I said, 'I have lost my way in the bush coming from the town, and I want some person to show me the way to the mill at the Falls.'

" 'Shure, thin,' she said, 'an' it's no time to be axin' tired men or the bhyes to be lavin' their beds, but sit ye down an' I'll speak to me man yonder,' And pointing to another couch where three boys of different ages were sleeping beside their father, she got up.

"After some discussion between them the master agreed to send one of the boys, as soon as it was light, to guide me to the Falls.

" 'There, misthress,' he said, 'ye may jist make yerself aisy now, an' lie down on the bed by my gal; she has the ague an' the fever, but sh's as quiet as a lamb an' will not disturb ye.'

"This was kind enough, but I preferred sitting before the fire on a block of wood, that served in lieu of a stool, to sharing the sick girl's bed or partaking of a meal of fried pork and potatoes which the woman offered to prepare for me. Then the couple left me to my own cogitations and the companionship of my dog Nelson.

"The one feeling uppermost in my mind was thankfulness for my present safety and shelter, rude as it was. The very novelty of the situation almost amused me; then graver thoughts arose as I looked about on the smoke-stained wall and unbarked rafters from which grey mosses and cobwebs hung in fanciful drapery above my head. I thought of my former home in Scotland, of my old life of pride and luxury, of my Canadian home. What a strange contrast did it present to my mind at that moment, the red flashing light of the blazing woodfire, now burning fiercely, illuminating every corner of the rude dwelling and showing the faces of the sleepers in their lowly beds.

"Close beside me lay the poor sick girl, whose fevered cheek and labored breathing excited my compassion, for what comfort could there be for either body or mind on that hard bed and among those rude surroundings. The chinkings (so I hear the people call these wedges of wood between the logs) had fallen out in many places, and the intervals had been stuffed with straw, old rags, moss and other rubbish, to keep out the cold wind. Anyone might have known from what country the inmates of the shanty came, even without hearing the brogue of the south of Ireland in their speech.

"Few and simple were the articles of household use. Two or three shelves made of unplaned boards held a few crockery cups and cracked saucers, some tin plates and mugs, and a battered tin teapot, minus a handle; a frying pan with a long handle, an iron pot and a bake kettle seemed to comprise all the cooking utensils.

"There was a barrel of flour and another of pork, an Irish spade which gleamed brightly beside an axe, a hoe and a gun, the last supported by two wooden pegs driven into the log wall.

"While I leaned my back against the sick girl's bed and thus occupied myself in making an inventory of the furnishings of the house, I fell fast asleep. So weary was I that I slept on till daylight, when I was roused by the rolling over of one of the logs on the hearth.

"Looking up, I was startled by the sight of mine host, whose keen, black eyes were bent on me with, as I thought, a sinister, inquisitive look, such that I shrunk affrighted from before him.

"In good truth, a more courageous person than I am might have been justified in feeling afraid had she been in a similar position, utterly helpless and alone. But my fear soon subsided, and I thought it was wisest to affect a courage that I hardly felt and to show perfect confidence, so I said with as cheerful an air as I could assume,

" 'You caught me napping, sir.'

"I remember the time in the days of my romance reading that I would have fancied myself quite a heroine and turned my honest old Irishman into a brigand, but my intercourse with the Irish immigrants has taught me that there is little cause for fearing them, and my husband tells me that their wild passions are chiefly roused by insult to their country or their religion, or when excited by spirituous liquor, and that such an act as robbing or murdering the stranger who seeks shelter under their roof is unheard of in Canada.

"The old man's frank, good-humored manner and pressing hospitality soon reassured me, and I would not have hesitated to take him as my guide

through the lonely woods. He told me, however, that his boy Mike knew
every step of the road, and he could trust him to take care of me and he'd
'be proud to do it.'

"The good woman soon bestirred herself to get breakfast, and I was
hungry enough to take a share in the 'praties and pork' and to drink a cup
of tea, though there was only maple sugar to sweeten it and no milk to
soften its harshness; but I had become used in my own home to privations
in food and many common comforts, as you well know.

"One by one the three ragged urchins came stealing shyly from their
bed ready dressed for the day, and I verily believe their garments did duty
instead of bedclothes. The boys, Mike, Patrick and Jonas, had all the same
smoke-dried skins, grey eyes and black hair, with a certain shrewd
expression in their faces that one often sees in the Irish cabins. They cast
furtive glances of wonder at the strange lady, but no one ventured to make
a remark at my appearance; they bestowed all their attention upon Nelson, coaxing him into friendship by giving him bits of meat and bread,
which no doubt were very acceptable to the hungry dog.

"I gave the woman a piece of silver, which she protested against receiving but accepted after a little persuasion, and, escorted by Michael,
reached home thoroughly tired but very glad to find all well, though anxious at my delay.

"Now I am resting, and I fear I have tired you with the long account of
my adventure, of which I can only say, 'All's well that ends well.' "[5]

ON THE ISLAND OF MINNEWAWA

It was a lovely summer day in July, 1893, when we took possession of Minnewawa, our island in Stony Lake. The little platform that had done duty as wharf the year before had floated from its moorings, but a strong hand soon helped to replace it and to put me on the level ground above the rocky shores. A little out of breath from the climb, I sat down on the steps of the veranda surrounding the house to rest and enjoy the beauty of the prospect.

The lake, with its wild wooded rocky shores and its many islands, lay before me. The latter were of all forms and sizes, from the tiny islet that was no more than a half-hidden rock against which the wavelets lifted themselves and broke softly, almost caressingly, to the large tree-clad island, with deeply-indented bays and overhanging vine-covered rocks. There were rugged, darkly furrowed masses of rock, without foliage save a few tufts of juniper, their sides covered with grey lichens, those pioneers of vegetation, giving them a time-worn, hoary appearance. One after another they stretched away, until Mount Julien rose like a crown upon the mainland beyond.

With pleasure I contemplated the varied beauties of wood and rock, island and forest-bounded lake, and to the eastward the red rocky crest of Eagle Mount. How I longed to revel in those fields of mosses that are fed and kept ever green by its many springs, and which carpet in mosaic-like patches the surface of the gneiss rock.

It was indeed a lovely place, and I congratulated my daughter on her choice of the site for our little cottage.

Everything was new, clean and fresh within the little domicile, and all without wild and picturesque—rocks, trees, hill and valley, wildflowers, ferns, shrubs and moss, and the pure, sweet scent of the pines over all, breathing health and strength.

If I were a doctor I would send my patients to live in a shanty under the pines.

Our house is a small one. On one side a branching oak, with its dark shining leaves, nearly covers the roof, on the other a tall pine and an oak shade the veranda.

The island rises in the centre, and to the south is thickly wooded with many noble trees. The shores are steep and precipitous. A deep channel on one side divides the higher and main potion of the island from the lofty wooded mounds to the eastward.

At high water, in the spring, this gully must be over-flowed from end to end, but just now it is quite dry and is strewn with the *débris* of fallen trees. The ground rises again beyond, but so abruptly rugged and steep that I look at it and fear even by the aid of hands and knees it would be inaccessible to the most adventurous climber. A bold promontory terminates the island on the north, a dangerous, precipitous place, but tempting one with the grand views it commands.

A tiny tenant had taken up its abode over the doorway of the house where a patch of dark-green moss first attracted my attention; then, with a hasty flutter of wings a pretty little mother bird popped down from it and sought safety on a stump among the pile of dark rocks in the hollow below the steps of the veranda.

I am not quite sure if the bird was a wood phoebe or not. The back and wing coverings were a dark slate; the head black, with some white about the breast; the legs dark and slender. Her nest was very neat and compact, made entirely of one sort of moss, and coated inside with mud. The eggs in it were small, round, whitish and speckled. The nearest description to it that I can find in Mr. McIlwraith's book is that of the Gnat-catcher, but I do not feel quite satisfied that my little lodger over the door was one of that family.

Ontario—Gore's Landing, View Showing Rice Lake and Paddle Steamer Northumberland, *1850,* by William A. Johnson.

It was very watchful and timid, yet bold to defend its nest, never ceasing to flit to and fro till it saw me moving away, when it darted back to the nest, and would not leave it, though in returning I passed through the doorway below the sill where it rested. I do not think it was a treecreeper, the legs were too long and slender; yet it seemed to cling to the stump when it lighted there, though without the backward movement peculiar to the treecreeper.

The little bird seemed very solitary, as I saw no mate, and one day while we were away the wary little mother took the opportunity of carrying off her brood. The nest was empty and the birds flown when we returned, and though we sought among the rocks and bushes we found no trace of them.

These birds are evidently fond of such shelters as sheds and under roofs, for in the old kitchen I found another nest of the same make and materials, but deserted, and at Fairy Lodge there was another neat new one of the same round deep pattern. Later, when staying at Fair Havens, the summer retreat of another of my daughters, I noticed a lively family of the same little bird associating with the little brown certhia and small downy woodpeckers. There was a company of four or five of these pretty birds, and they were so tame and fearless that they would alight from the overhanging branches of a pine tree that shadowed the platform of rock on which the house was built, and come down almost to my feet to take the crumbs I scattered for them. Then having enjoyed the feast, they retired to the tree to watch and wait for a fresh supply, readily sharing it with the other birds, with whom they seemed on the best of social terms.

There were sweet warbling notes, low and tender, uttered among them, but which were the musical birds of the flock I could not discover.

Blue harebells grow in the crevices of the rocks, and when in the canoe my companions are ever ready to indulge my covetous desires and to paddle close into the shore and climb the rocks to gather me the treasures.

How often in years long gone by have I gathered the lovely bluebell from among the heather, both in England and Scotland! How different the soil in which it flourishes here to the dry black sand of the heathlands there, yet the flowers seem just the same. Although I knew the species to be that of the *Campanula rotundifolia*, I had often questioned the correctness of the descriptive name, the root leaves being so little seen; but here they were all right, though withered. I had the whole plant—root, stem and flowers—and saw that the leaves were, or had been, round or rounded, so the botanists were right, and the flower deserved the specific name. Though faded, the foliage had fulfilled its office of caterer to the slender stems and delicate buds and blossoms. It might not render up to Mother Earth such earthy particles as had been borrowed from her to perfect the fair desert flowers. They had not need much—a little black mould, a rift in the dark rugged rock to hold them in position, the rain and the dews to nourish them, and the sunshine to tint the bells with a ray from the fountain of light.

Sweet flowers! Were ye indeed "born to blush unseen and waste your sweetness on the desert air?"[1] How can we tell? May not the gardens of the great Creator be realms of beauty to those who walk the earth unseen by man?

"Nor think though men were none,
   That heaven would want spectators, God want praise;
   Millions of spiritual creatures walk the earth
   Unseen, both when we wake and when we sleep;
   All these with ceaseless praise His works behold
      Both day and night."[2]

THE CHILDREN OF THE FOREST

ↄↄ

"Ye say they all have passed away,
That noble race and brave;
That their light canoes have vanished
From off the crested wave;
That in the forests where they roamed
There rings no hunter's shout,—
But their name is on your waters,
Ye may not wash it out."
—*L. Sigourney*[1]

JUDGING from the natural reticence of the dusky-skinned Indian, one would not suppose him capable of conceiving one poetical idea, yet under the stolid and apparently unimaginative exterior there lies a store of imagery, drawn from the natural objects around him, which he studies more carefully than we do our most interesting books. Nature is the only volume of knowledge to the child of the forest and plain. He borrows no ideas from written books. His Manito[u] the Great Spirit, the God of Nature, supplies all he needs. He seeks for no rhymes in which to clothe his simple thoughts, no flowery verse; but there is poetry in his speech, and a musical ring in the names he has given to the rivers, lakes and flowers that is absent in ours. The Indian names are both descriptive and characteristic, and in some instances contain the germ of local or distinctive history, which change or even mispronunciation would obliterate for ever.

The disjointed syllables may not sound euphonious to foreign ears, but to the understanding of the native Indian they convey a simple description, a graphic word-picture. The beautiful rapid Otonabee is described in the name, "water running swiftly flashing brightly;" Katchewanook, "lake of three islands;" Ontario, "sheet of placid water;" Pem-a-dash-dakota, "lake of the burning plains," the original name of Rice Lake. How many years ago it was that these plains were burned over they do not know, but that they were the scene of a great conflagration the Indian name, as well as the half-charred blackened roots below the surface of the soil, prove. Napanee, the Indian word for flour, indicates that on the site of that now flourishing town the first flour mills in the district were erected.

How much prettier is the Indian name for Spring Beauty, "Mis-ko-deed," than the unmeaning botanical one of *Claytonia Virginica*. In the latter some botanist has perpetuated his own insignificant name of Clayton, while the Indian mother, with truer instinct, though she might give the name Mis-ko-deed to her April-born child, would never name a flower after her child.

The Indian girl's name, Mad-wa-osha, is harsh on our tongue until we render it into English in "murmuring winds." The Indians were always good friends to me, and I have ever taken a great interest in and sympathized with them, admiring their patience and quiet endurance under great privations.

Would that the charitably disposed, who do so much for the poor in the large cities, would turn their thoughts more often to the suffering among the scattered remnant of the former owners of the land! The men, restricted by the narrow limits of civilization, die early, leaving widows and orphans, or linger out a dull existence by the fireside, their blood grown sluggish, and their one-time energy in the chase weakened by the necessary observance of the game laws. Those of the last generation have lost their spirit; the boys of the present have nothing to call theirs into active existence. I once asked an Indian woman in the village what the great boys I saw lounging about the streets did. "They? Eat!" was the terse and emphatic reply.

But I am wandering away from the Indian names. The one given me, Peta-wan-noo-ka, "red cloud of the dawn," was suggested by my rosy English complexion, and those given to others among the early settlers in the bush were equally poetical or descriptive.

What a pity it is that the meanings of all the Indian names, remaining to our lakes, rivers or cities are not understood and made familiar; and greater pity still, that is some cases they have been set aside to make room for European names that have no significance to Canadians.

About four miles above Stony Lake there is a shallow piece of water known to the settlers by the name of Bowshink. This lake (though it hardly deserves the term) lies below the highest elevation of land, in that section, called "Jack's Mountain," famous for its deposits of mica and other minerals. Seen through its embossing mass of forest trees, the eye takes in little beyond the silvery gleam of the water visible at intervals between the trees.

Chippewa Indians, Rama Indian Reserve, Ontario, September 1876, by George Harlow White.

One of the settlers, who was curious about the origin of the Indian nomenclature, asked what the words *Bow-shink* signified.

"Spilt water; looks like it," replied the Indian, Moses Muskrat, as he stalked away, laughing at the conceit.

The words of lamentation for the dead, "*Wah-ha-no-min,*" when uttered by them in a long drawn-out mournful cadence and minor key, have an indescribable wailing sound of grief and woe.

Ty-zah, spoken quickly with an upward inflection of the voice, are excellent expressions of the combined wonder, admiration and surprise the words are meant to convey; and the low monotonous sounds, *Ha-ha-ho-ho-hi-hi*, varied only by the transposing of the syllables, and accompanied by a slow movement of the body, a sort of rocking to and fro, is a soothing sleep-inducing cradlesong, which grows as one listens into a semblance of the sighing sound of the summer wind among the pine tops.

There is a dry humor, too, shown in some of their names. "The-Man-with-Two-Tongues" is, I think, an excellent *sobriquet* for a liar or deceiver, a character greatly despised by the Indian. "The-Man-who-Walks-Under-the-Dirt" may be taken to mean a miner, but it has possibly an allegorical and deeper significance to their ears.

Their code of morality is quite as well defined as in our own decalogue, but is, of course, not more strictly kept by the bad Indian than our own by the bad white man who disgraces the name of Christian.

Their laws are few and simple, suited to the savage for the protection of life and property between man and man. Theft, lying, murder—that is, taking life without justifiable cause—comprise the criminal code.

Their religion was pantheistic before evangelization, and the older people in the Rice Lake district held a vague belief in a great and good Spirit, an overruling Deity; but even this knowledge was dim and was limited to such as were under the influence of their wise or "medicine" men. They had a general belief in the power of demons or inferior spirits who ruled the elements of water, earth and air. These were their Lares and Penates,[2] like the household gods of the heathen Greeks and Romans, but the Indians made no graven images or idols to represent these imaginary spirits. They gave propitiatory offerings of food or drink to avert their displeasure, or as thanks for favors received, and before meals a morsel cast from their hand or a few drops of liquid were thus given as a sort of silent grace, but the custom is now no longer seen among the Christian Indians.

It is seventy years since the work of evangelizing the Indians of this part of Ontario was begun through the efforts of the missionaries, and it has pleased God's Spirit to bless their labors. All honor to the devoted men who labored so faithfully to preach the Gospel of Christ to the red men, to bring them out of darkness into the blessed light of love and everlasting life. With the simplicity of children they have received the truth and kept it.

The little hamlet of Hiawatha, on the north shore of Rice Lake, sent forth Peter Jacobs, John Sunday and others whose names are not so familiar to me—earnest Christian workers to carry the Word to the red men of other tribes.

Some few years ago the Reverend Dr. Bethune (not our respected late Bishop, though bearing the same name, but the Lutheran Bishop of Brooklyn, U.S.) was on a visit to a family residing on the south side of Rice Lake, opposite to the little Indian village. The Doctor, in the early years of his ministry, had been a teacher and evangelizer of the Indians, and loved the work.

In reply to a neighboring cleryman's complaint of the difficulty of reaching the understanding of the Indians and of breaking through their stolid indifference, he said,

"Ah, my friend, you do not go the right way to work. You must reach the Indian through *his* knowledge, not through *yours*, from the word pictures written in the only book he knows, the book of Nature."

On Sunday morning at an early hour Doctor Bethune crossed the lake to preach to the Indians, and was met on the shore by the leading men.

One of them—it might have been John Sunday, or George Copway, or Tobico—asked the Doctor to explain the work of the Holy Spirit in giving light to the soul, an enquiry which elicited the following brief but effective sermon:—

"My Indian brother, look at the lake before you."

The Indians uttered a groan-like "Ugh!" They could not see the water—lake and sunlight alike were obscured by a thick fog. They gazed upon it, no one speaking. The preacher bent his head in silent prayer.

Suddenly a light wind, stirring the air, breathed upon the mist, and as if by some magical touch the dense curtain began to rise, and slowly rolling back to the hills and treetops, allowed the sun in all its morning splendor to shed its light upon the little band of expectant worshippers. Then the preacher, lifting his hand, said: "Even as the rays of yon sun break through the dense mists that hid his face and the dark waters of the lake below from your sight, so the Spirit of the blessed Lord Jesus, the Son of God, shines down into the hearts of men, showing the dark waters of sin and lifting the cloud which hid from them all the goodness and power and mercy of their Father who is in Heaven. This light is life. 'Let the wicked forsake his way, and the unrighteous man his thoughts; and let him return unto the Lord, and he will have mercy upon him; and to our God, for he will abundantly pardon.'[3] My Indian brothers, let us pray."

"The preacher's words are good; your Indian brothers see light in them," was the hearty response to this simple and beautiful discourse.

> "In Nature's book on lake and stream,
>   And flower-strewn path, and isle untrod
> By pale-face feet, the red man reads
>   The word of the eternal God.
> The dawn to him a promise gives,
>   The day the looked-for gift bestows;
> He reads the signs, by reason lives
>   His part to do—for well he knows
> That Nature fails not nor deceives—
>   Trusts the Great Spirit and believes."[4]

THOUGHTS ON VEGETABLE INSTINCT

THE GREAT Creator has endowed all vegetables with a property analogous to life and sensation. The plant, like the animal, is subject to the law of death and decay. This very fact is a proof of life, for that which has not life cannot be said to die.

Differing from the animal, we still find in the plant an inanimate power exerted for its preservation. This power, which might be termed Vegetable Instinct, seems even in the plant an approach to the exercise of will, though in a very limited degree. This may be instanced in its selection or rejection of such nutriment as is suitable or detrimental to its growth.

The tree, indeed, is not gifted with volition to change its place, as the animal or even the insect can do; it cannot come and go, but it can refuse to grow and flourish where it has been planted, should soil or climate prove foreign to its nature. It shows, as it were, a will of its own, which is often stubborn and resists interference from man's will; and man must conform as far as it is possible to the natural wants of the tree or the plant if he would turn it to his own advantage.

The vegetable, like the animal, experiences hunger, and must be fed. Like the animal, also, it seems to be endowed with a power of choice. It has its likings and disliking; it rejects or selects according to its peculiar tastes and necessities.

Squirrel Corn, Purple Trillium, Wild Crane's Bill, Star
Flower Chickweed, by Agnes FitzGibbon, in *Canadian*
Wild Flowers (1868).

Man by his superior gifts can, by care and observation, give to the plant
what is needful to promote its growth, and by long experience is enabled
to acclimatize, improve, and, as it were, educate the plant for his own uses,
through the power given him by God.

The florist or the agriculturist is able to increase the value of his crops
by studying the best food for the plants whose seed he casts into the
ground. Yet, that there is a diversity in the requirements of some vegetables is evident. Some species are gross and demand rich soil; others of a
more delicate habit are abstemious, and will thrive best with the most
scanty nourishment, where the ranker feeding kinds would starve.

The little Carpet Weed, a small hardy plant belonging to the Poligon-
um family, grows and thrives by our path in dry sandy soil; down-trodden
and despised it still flowers and increases, where another species would
perish utterly. In richer mould and under the protecting hand of culture,
this sturdy little plant might dwindle away and lose its hardihood.

There are marvels of beauty among the Orchids, which feed upon what the atmosphere alone supplies. These floral beauties, dressed in the most glorious colors, seem to be fed by air and sunbeams, the gifts of Him who made their forms so wondrous fair and caused their seed, invisible to our eyes, to fall upon some sapless branch, or wall, or rugged rock, there to grow and flourish and die, perhaps never looked upon by the eye of man.[1]

Is it not wonderful how these lovely orchids grow and thrive, and drink in the dews of heaven, expanding their petals to receive the light and warmth, to become living manifestations of the wisdom and goodness of Him who made them for His glory and His pleasure, and fed them by His care to delight other eyes than ours?[2]

It is true that in virtue of the authority vested in man, he can subject in some measure the vegetable world to his use. He was given power to subdue the earth and govern it. That was his privilege during his state of obedience, but now the earth is rebellious and it requires labor to govern it and to restore that which was cursed for his sake. The thorns and thistles must be rooted up or the land will not yield to him its strength. Labor is the remedy, and man must exert both bodily strength and mental skill to live. The life-supporting grain must be cultivated; it will not yield its substance spontaneously. So Christ is the remedy for the moral weeds sown by our spiritual foe.

That the plant possesses an energy within itself to overcome obstacles that interfere with its growth may be noticed. I have seen an elm or beech embracing with its strong elastic roots a huge block of stone, binding it down while it sent out its smaller fibrous rootlets to the soil below. The tree itself had sprung into life from a seed that had fallen into a crevice of the rugged stone, but as it advanced in stature it required more support and more nutriment. Firmly rooted, it now defied the force of wind and storm. It threw out its cables and its anchors, and then began to flourish more abundantly—not by the large woody roots, but by the tender vegetable tubes drinking up the food from the more generous soil which they had entered to wait upon and feed the tree, like faithful servants ready to cater to their masters' wants.

There is power in the living germ of a tiny seed. See how the tender blade of wheat will pierce the hardest clod. The seedling of some delicate flower will burst through the environing mould, raising its soft plumy leaflets to the light and air, while sending down its roots deep into the earth, exerting a force from within its tender frame that eludes the most cunning scrutiny of the eye to detect. Silently and secretly this mysterious action takes place in the sprouting seed. The sceptic says, "It is the necessity of its nature." True, but the sceptic does not see God in Nature.

There is a curious adaptation in plants to overcome certain obstacles that obstruct their progress in growth, and that enables them to put forth certain energies which under other circumstances are not exerted.

This is seen in the case of the ivy and many other climbing plants. In its infant stage the ivy appears as a tender light green plant, with sharply pointed leaves. For a time it creeps over the ground; then when more advanced, the leaves take a lobed form and become of a dark green, the stem woody and branching. The slender branchlets seeking support, it raises itself to any elevation from the ground, by means of some bush or the trunk of a tree. It puts forth tiny flat feet, armed with imperceptible rootlets, by which it attaches itself to the rough surface of a wall or the bark of a tree. It may be for shelter or support, it cannot be for nourishment. It is not improbable that climbing is inherent in its nature, and so it strives to overcome every obstacle that interferes with its upward progress—who shall say?—and to this end it exerts, to accomplish its desire, a power that it had no need to make use of in its former condition.

The sower who casts his seed in the furrows of his field never pauses to think how it will fall—whether or not it shall lie in the best position for the germination of the grain.

Nature follows her own laws without heed to the hand that sows the seed. The latter will right itself. Place a bulb in the earth with the crown downward or sideways, and it will come up in spite of the awkward position it was planted in.

Here are a number of onions or of potatoes left lying in all manner of ways; the shoots, you will notice, take the upward direction attracted to the light. The innate power in the living vegetable is to ascend to the light, while the root descends, loving darkness rather than light.

Thus the inanimate things of creation silently obey the will of the Creator, fulfilling the work which He has ordained to His praise and glory. He hath given them laws which shall not be broken.

A FLORAL MYSTERY

An interesting account of the peculiar properties of some aquatic plants, as illustrative of what we have called vegetable instinct, may not be out of place here, and will perhaps be new to some of my youthful readers.

Michelet,[3] the delightful old French naturalist, gives the following history of the *Vallisneria*, better known by its common name of Tape or Eel Grass, an aquatic plant very frequently seen in slow-flowing lakes and ponds, covering the surface during the latter part of the summer with its slender light green leaves and white floating flowers:

"The blossoms of this water plant are of two kinds. The stamens or pollen-bearing flowers are clustered on short scapes (stems), and are seen growing at the bottom of the lake or pond. The fertile or fruit-bearing blossoms, on long thready elastic stalks, rise to the surface of the water, and there expand to await the appearance of the sterile or male flower, the buds of which break away from the bottom of their watery bed and float upwards, open out their petals, and, mingling with the fertile flowers, shed upon them the fertilizing pollen dust. The latter after awhile retire below the surface by means of the spirally coiled scape, which by contracting, draws down the impregnated flower, there to ripen and perfect its seed. The seed vessel, which is a very long and slender pod, of an olive brown color, is attached to the stalk of the female flower."

The pretty white blossoms of this singular plant are about the size of a quarter-dollar, and in the month of August the flowers may be seen in some quiet bay, covering the still waters with their snowy petals.

THE WHITE WATER LILY

The beautiful Water Lily,* that "Queen of the Lakes," what pen can do justice to her loveliness![4]

The exquisitely folded buds are seen at all stages of development, rising midway from the bed of the still waters as you look downward into its depth. As they reach the influence of the light and the warm sunshine, the flowers expand into full-blown beauty and delicious lemon-scented fragrance.

Nymphœ Oderata.

To float beside a bed of these beautiful flowers and glossy widespread leaves is a treat not to be forgotten. As daylight closes to evening, the lovely blossoms fold their snowy petals over the golden stamens and retire to their watery chambers for the night.

The native water lilies of North America exceed in size and beauty those of England, and there are varieties found among our inland lakes in Ontario, tinged with the most delicate rose pink.* I have seen, in one of the inland lakes, a very small and lovely water lily hardly exceeding a silver dollar in size.

In many aquatic plants we find the foliage is minutely and finely divided, which enables the water to flow through them without any impediment, as in the Pondweed Family. In the water *Ranunculi* the root leaves are flat and wide-spreading, but as the plant ascends the leaves are cut into fine, narrow segments, and so allow the currents of water to pass freely through them.

---

*In my "Studies of Plant Life," illustrated by Mrs. Chamberlin, is given a colored plate of the pink *Nymphoe Oderata*.

SOME CURIOUS PLANTS

BROOM RAPE

AMONG the wild vegetable products of our forests may be found many strange-looking plants unlike any of those with which we are familiar in our gardens or fields.

One of these is the Broom Rape (*Orobanche*). It comes up in the woods, often by the pathway, and at first glance you take it for a little bundle of hard dry brown twigs, but on closer inspection you see that it is a plant with life and growth in it.

The stems are clustered together at the base. It can hardly be said to have any roots, and yet it is bearing its flowers almost underground as well as upon its scaly stems. Of foliage it has none, at least no green leaves, only scales dry and brown, and the flowers are simply two little hard-beaked, bead-shaped scales, made noticeable by the abundance of yellowish stamens and anthers which look like little heaps of sawdust. The stigmas are not visible. The whole plant looks like a tiny brush or broom, and it more remarkable for the oddity of its appearance than for its beauty.

It belongs to a singular family, that known as the *Orobanche* or Broom Rape family, to which also the term Cancer Root has been popularly given. I believe this curious plant is used by the Indian herb doctor as a cure for cancer, but whether outwardly or inwardly is not known.

There are several species, some of the order having blue and white tubular flowers, others yellowish-brown and hairy; all are parasites on the roots of oak, beech and some other trees.

INDIAN PIPE

Another of our curious flowers is the Indian Pipe (*Monotropa uniflora*). This singular plant is distinguished by its pure whiteness, without one tinge of color. From root to summit it is spotless, white as new fallen snow. It is also called the Wood Snowdrop. It attracts the eye by its contrast to the dark rich mould on which it grows, generally at the foot of beech trees, sending up a cluster of white-scaled stems some nine or ten inches in height. Each thick stem is terminated by one white pellucid flower about the size of a small tobacco pipe, the head slightly bent downward at first, but becoming erect for the better preservation of the seed.

So sensitive is this remarkable plant that it turns black soon after being pulled, as if polluted by contact with the human hand. In the herbarium it loses all its beauty, turning black as ink, nor can it retain its semi-transparent texture. To appreciate the plant it must be seen growing in the shade of the forest.

There is another species, found only in pine and evergreen woods, which is of a tawny color, the stem woolly and bearing from three to five flowers. The bells, when upright, are filled with drops of clear honey.

This is known as Sweet Pine Sap. Like the *uniflora* the Pine Sap (*Monotropa hypopitys*) is a perfect flower and not a fungous growth, as some have supposed. It also is leafless, the foliage being mere thin scales arranged along the scape.

THE DODDER

The Dodder (*Cuscuta*) is another of our eccentric plants, of which we have several native species.

The singularity of one of these struck me as very remarkable, from the attachment it showed for one particular plant, a slender species of Goldenrod. There were other plants growing near these Dodders which would have given all the needed support, but they evidently did not possess the same attraction and were passed by—it was the little Solidago and none other. It really looked like *will* in the Dodders.

And what was strange, too, both plants seemed perfectly healthy—while the clustered flowers of the Dodder coiled round the supporting stem of the Goldenrod, the latter bore its yellow blossoms fresh and fair to view uninjured. I preserved several specimens of the united flowers for my herbal.

The stem of the Dodder was leafless, of a rather rusty green, hard and wiry; the numerous clusters of flowers were greenish white.

Another species of this curious plant, with thready orange-colored coils, I found on the rocks twining among grasses and other herbage.

SENSITIVE PLANTS

There are certain flowers, the floral organs of which are so sensitive that the slightest touch affects them.

This sensibility, though differing from what I have called vegetable instinct, seems to indicate a sense of feeling akin to a life principle existing in the flower. Possibly the more learned naturalist may object to my crude idea on this most interesting subject. I know little beyond what observation teaches or suggests, and am open to correction when I err. My main object in these pages has been to awaken an interest in young readers, such as to induce them to seek and learn for themselves. Knowledge thus gained is very pleasant and leads upward and onward to higher and more satisfactory results.

Everyone knows the nervous sensitiveness of the leaves of the Sensitive Plant, which on the slightest touch from the finger instantly closes and collapses as if fainting; but it is not of this and others of a similar nature that I wish to remark, but of a few of our native flowers.

There is the not uncommon shrub, the Berberry, the blossoms of which can easily be tested. If the base of the stamens is touched with a pin or needle they instantly close together. Probably a similar effect is produced by the tongue of the bee or the sucker of a fly. Not only to scatter the pollen dust, but it may be to guard the germen of the flower from injury, that this movement of the stamens takes place.

The same effect seems to be produced in the sensitive organs of the flowers of that pretty shrub known as Dogbane[1] (*Apocynum androsœmifolium*) or shrubby Milkweed. The little pink-striped blossoms of this plant seem to be chosen by some species of very small fly as a sleeping place (that is, if flies do sleep). As evening dews begin to fall they resort to the sweet-scented bells for rest or shelter, but are instantly captured by the flower stamens, as may be seen by the closed anther tips. In every bell a tiny prisoner is held fast in the tenacious clasp of the organs of the flower.

It has been a matter of dispute whether the Pitcher Plant (*Sarracenia Purpurea*) feeds upon the insects that creep within its hollow tube-like leaves or not. That the insects, flies or beetles, enter either for shelter or for the fluids contained in these beautiful natural vases seems most likely, and having entered, the still, reflexed hairs that line the tubes form a barrier to their exit. The consequence is that they are either drowned, which is most probably their fate, or made prisoners for life. The trap proves fatal to the unwary flies, but the plant can in nowise be answerable for their death. They had no business to intrude themselves uninvited on the premises, and so there can be no case of wilful murder against the pitcher plants. The verdict is "accidental death," and an impartial jury, could such be called, would say, "Serves them right! what business had they there?"

Nor can it be proved that the plants derive any benefit from the intrusion of the insects otherwise than that all vegetables feed on the carbonic exhalations arising from decomposing animal or vegetable matter.

The pitcher plant is the northern representative of a most remarkable order. It occurs both in Canada and all over the continent of North America, and if not so wonderful in appearance as some of the magnificent tropical species, it is too singular in structure and habits to be passed by without notice.

Well worth seeing, indeed, is a bed of pitcher plants, especially in the month of June, their flowering time.

The tall, naked scape bears one large deep red blossom. From the globular five-rayed ovary rises a short, pillar-like style which expands into a thin yellow umbrella-shaped body, elegantly scalloped at the edges and covering the floral organs, adding greatly to the beauty of the flower.

All the parts of the flower are in fives—petals, sepals and valves of the seed vessel. The root is thick and fleshy, the hollow leaves beautifully veined with bright crimson; the lip or mouth of the leaves is scalloped and the interior fringed with stiff, silvery hairs.

Following the inner part of each leaf runs a membrane like a flap. This curious appendage, being shorter than the outside curve of the leaf, throws the hollow mouth into the right position for receiving and retaining the water with which the pitcher is generally half filled.

In some species of this most interesting order of plants there is a natural lid which probably answers the same purpose. In some the urn or pitcher is a prolongation of the leaf, and is suspended by a tendril. The flower, which is distinct from the curious hollow leaf, fades quickly and bears an abundance of seed. The whole plant is singular in all its parts, and is a sight to be admired.

SOME VARIETIES OF POLLEN

THE fertilizing dust or pollen of different flowers varies in shape, no two species being exactly alike when examined under a powerful microscope.

As the subject may have hitherto escaped the attention of my readers, I will notice what varieties have been perceived and made note of by such scientific naturalists as Jussieu,[1] Malpighi[2] and others.

Malpighi, the learned French naturalist, found that the pollen of the sunflower was round, but beset with rough prickles; in the cranesbill or geranium family the particles were perforated; in the mallow they took the form of wheels with teeth; in the palma Christi, like grains of wheat; in pansies, angular; in maize or Indian corn, flat and smooth; in borage, like a thin rolled-up leaf; in coniferae, double globules.

The observations of Jussieu concerning the pollen of the maple deserves our notice. He says: "Those gentlemen who have minutely examined the fertilizing dust of the flower of the maple, have drawn the figure of the particles in the form of a cross, but I find them to be globular; nevertheless, as soon as they were touched with moisture they instantly burst into four parts, assuming the form of the cross.

"From which it may be inferred that the hollow globules contained some subtle fluid which, when moistened by rain or dew, burst and discharged their contents on the surrounding organs of the flower."—*Evelyn's Silva.*[3]

What wondrous secrets are revealed to us through the medium of the microscope! What a world of interest does it open to the inquiring mind of the young student of Nature!

The minutest insect, the wing of a fly, a drop of puddle water, the capsule of a tiny moss, or a morsel of seaweed, are revelations sealed to the mere outward, unassisted vision.

A scientist once remarked, "Life, even a long life, is not long enough to take in the thousandth part of what wonders the microscope could reveal to us in one short hour, of things so insignificant that we pass them by without seeing or caring for them."[4]

There is nothing small in God's sight. To us these things may appear insignificant, but all have been created with a purpose, and go to complete the wonderful work of the creation.

POLLEN OF THE WHITE PINE

When I first settled in the backwoods of northern Ontario, I noticed that after heavy thunderstorms the water on the surface of the lake and the puddles on the ground were covered with a fine sulphur-colored powdery substance, which lay like a thin yellow crust on the earth after the water had evaporated. On asking an old settler what it was, he answered, "Sulphur, which comes down with the rain from the clouds. We call them sulphur showers, for it is always seen in this country after thunderstorms."

Not being quite convinced of the real nature of the substance, I collected a portion of it, dried it and forwarded it to a friend who was the possessor of a fine microscope of four hundred magnifying power. I received from him a drawing of the magnified powder grains, which resembled grains of wheat, a central line dividing the figure, giving the idea of duality to the form of each atom.

My friend pronounced the substance to be the pollen of the White or Weymouth Pine (*Pinus strobus*).

This settled the matter and was perfectly conclusive, especially as this sulphur-looking substance is seen only during the time when the cone-bearing trees are in flower in July, which is also the time when thunderstorms are most general.

The extreme lightness of the pollen dust renders it probable that it may ascend into the upper air or cloud region, and be precipitated to the earth during heavy showers.

It is a curious and, if needed, a convincing fact, that this phenomenon is rarely, if ever, noticed now in the cleared parts of the country. This may be attributed to the great destruction of the pines, the forests in many places being denuded almost to the extermination of these noble trees. The time, indeed, seems fast approaching when the pine tribe will disappear and become a thing of the past only.

While writing on the subject of the so-called "Sulphur Showers," I was much pleased and surprised by reading a passage I met with quite unexpectedly in a volume of that rare and interesting book, *Evelyn's Sylva*. It is so much to the purpose that I will transcribe it. The writer observes:

"The figure of each of the minute particles which form so important a part in the economy of every plant and tree, probably varies in shape in each tribe, even in the various species.

"To the unassisted eye we see only a fine yellow or grey dust that floats so lightly on the air that the least breath of wind ruffling the branches moves it, and so light and so plentiful is the supply that, if it chances to rain during the flowering season of the pines, the standing waters near will be painted with the yellow rings of this dust from the trees."

It is known that the mingling of pollen from flowers of the same natural order, through the agency of bees and other winged insects, is the cause of the great variety of species which we find in plants of the same family; thus the different races of plants can be traced back to their natural orders, including the genus and species of every family in all its variations.

THE CRANBERRY MARSH

To THE EYE of the botanist our cranberry marshes are fields of beauty and of great interest.

Elegant wreaths of this beautiful evergreen plant, with its tiny dark green, glossy leaves, trail over lovely peat mosses, the *Sphagnum cymbefolium* and the *Sphagnum ciliare*.

The delicate pink bells, pendent on their light thready stalks, are seen through the season with the fruit in every stage of growth and color, from the tiny dot not larger than the head of a pin to the pear-shaped, full-sized berry, green, yellow and bright purplish-red, hanging among the soft, creamy mosses; and, often, over all, a forest of the stately chain fern or the noble *Osmundi regalis*, both of which love the moisture of the peat soil and the cranberry marsh.

Theses marshes are the nurseries of many other varieties of ferns, flow ers, orchids, plants and shrubs. They are also the haunts of harmless species of snakes, for although the black snake and the copperhead have rather a doubtful reputation, I have never yet heard of any injury being suffered from these obnoxious reptiles.

All sorts of flies are bred in these marshy places—mosquitoes, deer-flies and big gadflies (the terror of cattle in the Northwest, under the name of "bulldogs"), and most likely those little torments, the Canadian black-flies, may nestle there, too. Owing to this rather undesirable company, the lovely wild garden is rather shunned by the timid botanist during the months of May and June, when it puts forth its greatest attractions in flowers and shrubs.

To enter into this paradise of wild flowers and flies, moths and beetles, the naturalist must not be afraid of mosquitoes or wet feet, nor must he mind tripping in a hidden network of tangled roots. Such accidents will not hurt him, and if he is an enthusiastic botanist or entomologist, he will laugh at such trifling matters and scramble on in spite of black snakes or bullfrogs, to be rewarded by finding many a rare bog orchid, unobtainable upon the dusty highways and byways among the common haunts of men.

Just fancy a young field naturalist returning from an exploring tour in the cranberry marsh. He is hot and tired, a good deal fly-bitten, dilapidated in dress and appearance, somewhat the worse for wear, but with looks that tell of unexpected good fortune.

Having hastily satisfied his hunger and thirst at the camp, he unstraps his japanned[1] case, and, his face beaming with triumphant smiles, proceeds to exhibit his wonderful finds in the shape of rare beetles of metallic hues, green, red, scarlet, blue and sulphur-colored; dragonflies large and small, bronze, blue, red or metallic green; silvery moths with dappled wings or elegant blue ones with brilliant eyes.

From a little pillbox which he has carried carefully in his vest pocket he takes a tiny land tortoise, no bigger than a black beetle, that he found basking in the sand near a creek and only just hatched from its warm shady nest.

And then he will be off the next morning at sunrise to the big peat moss which he has not yet had leisure to explore.

The peat mosses are, of all our native mosses, the most worthy of notice. They form extensive beds, many acres in extent, in overflowed marshes, extinct lakes and partially dried beaver meadows, where the bottom soil is still wet and spongy.

In such situations where these white mosses abound, mingled with the running vines of the cranberry there are other marsh-loving plants and shrubs, such as the Labrador Tea (*Ledum latifolia*), the Wild Rosemary (*Andromeda polifolia*), the Kalmia and the white and pink flowered Spiraea.

Here, too, we meet with large beds of the curious and interesting pitcher plants and that little gem, the sundew. The leaves of this latter plant are round in form, of a red color, the edges beset with pellucid, shining drops, reflecting the rays of light like diamonds. There are two species, the *Drosera rotundifolia* and the *Drosera longifolia*. The flowers are small and white, sometimes tinged with pink and borne on tall stems. The former is the prettier of the two. In such places, also, we find some of our rarest orchids—the Grass Pink (*Colopogen pulchellus*), the stemless Lady's Slipper (*Cyprepedium acaule*), the Ram's Head Orchid (*C. aristenum*), the Arethusa; the *Calypso borealis*, or Bird's Eye Orchid, and many others.

When very young the peat moss is of the liveliest tender green, but as it increases in growth it becomes of a creamy whiteness, which deepens again with age to soft rose pink, the fruitful plant turning to a deep rose purple and the bud-like capsules collecting at the summit.

The foliage of the larger species is soft and cottony, drooping or flaccid, densely clothing the upright stems, which in height often measure from nine inches to a foot, and being interwoven, support each other, forming deep, soft beds.

Nor are the peat mosses without their uses. They are so soft and pliable that they are found most serviceable to the florist, nurseryman and gardener as a suitable material for packing the roots of plants and shrubs for distant transportation, for which purpose many tons are used in the year.

There are several species of sphagnums. The slender, delicate *S. acutifolium* has narrower leaves than the *S. cymbefolium*. The capsules are green, not red, and the plant is not so robust, but it is still curious and fair to look upon.

Many other kinds of coarse mosses also mingle with the sphagnums and form pleasing contrasts to the whiter mosses and bog-loving plants.

OUR NATIVE GRASSES

"And the blithe grass blades that stand straight up
And make themselves small, to leave room for all
    The nameless blossoms that nestle between
    Their sheltering stems in the herbage green;
    Sharp little soldiers, trusty and true,
    Side by side in good order due;
    Arms straight down, and heads forward set,
    And saucily-pointed bayonet,
    Up the hillocks, and down again,
    The green grass marches into the plain,
    If only a light wind over the land
    Whispers the welcome word of command."
                  —Lord Lytton[1]

MODERN botanists have separated the old natural order of the grasses into three distinct divisions—the grass proper, *Gramineœ*; the sedges, *Cyperaceœ*; the rushes, *Juncaceoe*. But my knowledge of them is according to the old school, which included all in one great order. The stately, gigantic bamboo of the tropics; the sugar cane, the flexible canebrake of the southern swamps; the useful broom cane; the graceful feathery plumed grass of the Pampas, waving in the breeze like gently-heaving billows of a silvery shining sea; the heavy dark-headed bulrush so familiar to the

eye; the verdant rice and the purple-topped Indian corn with its silky tassels and golden fruit—all these, and the coarse grasses that grow on every
wild, uncultivated spot, rushes, reeds and sedges—all and every species
were classed with the sweet vernal grasses of the meadows and pasture;
from the highest to the lowest, they were all included under the familiar
name of Grass.

Ontario—Gore's Landing, St. George's Anglican Church, 1850, by William A. Johnson.

The rich variety and abundance of the native grasses of the western and
northwestern prairies of this great American continent form one of its most
attractive features—great waving oceans of verdure where the bison once
fed, but which are now yielding to the plow of the settler. Man by his reck-
less greed has driven off and well-nigh exterminated the bison (Indian
buffalo) from the plains of Manitoba and the Saskatchewan, and the wild
grasses of the prairie are also destined to disappear with the wild herds
which fed upon them.

It is a singular fact that among all the many varieties of the prairie grasses there are no true grain-bearing cereals to be found, none producing seed
sufficiently nutritive for the support of man. Although many of the grasses resemble oats, wheat, barley and maize, there seems to be in the substance they produce an absence of the qualities required to make bread.

The most edible grain that we find in a wild state is the *Zizania aquatica*, or "Water Oats"—the Indian rice—but it is not a native of the prairies, and is not found in many of the inland lakes of our Northwest, though abundant in the slow flowing waters of Ontario.

It grows in many of the upper lakes in such large beds as to resemble islands, and in the shallow bays and coves attains so rank a growth as to impede the passage of boats. When in flower it is one of the most graceful and lovely of our native grasses. The long flexible ribbon-like leaves float loosely on the surface of the water, and the tall spikes of the pretty straw-colored and purple anthers, freed from the fold of the slender stalks, hang gracefully fluttering in the breeze.

When the leaves turn yellow, and the grain ripens in the mellow days of late September or October, the Indian women gather it into their canoes by means of a short thin-bladed paddle, with which they strike the heads of the grain-bearing stalks against a stick held in the other hand and over the edge of the canoe.

The wild rice has a peculiar weedy, smoky flavor, but if properly cooked is very delicious. The Indians preserve it in many ways, and look upon it as belonging especially to them. They call the month of the rice harvest the "Moon of the Ripe Rice."

One of my Indian friends always brings me each year a pretty birch-bark basket of wild rice, giving it to me with the kindly words, spoken in her own soft tongue, "Present for you."

These little offerings are very sweet to me. They are genuine tokens of simple gratitude and affection, and for which I never offer any payment, knowing it would be at once rejected, for the rice is a free-will gift and therefore priceless.

The deer, too, feed upon the rice beds. The doe leads down her fawn to the lake, and the sweet, tender grassy leaves of the young rice are eaten eagerly by the gentle creature. In the season countless wildfowl come from the colder regions of the north, and the sportsmen know their favorite feeding beds among the rice fields of the inland lakes.

There is a beautiful chapter on "Grass" in the Rev. Hugh McMillan's charming volume, *Bible Teaching in Nature*,[2] which I wish everyone could read. I would gladly transcribe much of it, but would not thus rob my readers of the pleasure of enjoying the book for themselves. A few words only I must quote here:

"Grass forms the beautiful and appropriate covering of the grave. As it was the earth's first blessing, so it is her last legacy to man. The body that it fed when living, it reverently covers when dead with a garment richer than the robe of a king.

"When all other kindness in food and clothing and emblematical teaching is over, it takes up its Rizpah[3] watch beside the tomb, and forsakes not what all else has forsaken. Gently does it wrap up the ashes of the dead, wreathing like a laurel crown the cold damp brow with its interlacing roots, drawing down to the darkness and solitude of the grave the warm bright sunshine and blessed dews of heaven."

There is many an unknown grave in Canada long deserted and forgotten. In the early days of the colony the settlers were wont to bury their dead in some spot set apart as a family burying ground. There was little attention paid to the rites of religion, and little ceremony, for the dwellers were few, and their houses often far apart—some on the banks of lonely forest streams, others near the great lakes, and some deep-seated in the heart of the woods.

A prayer, maybe a hymn or psalm, a mother's tears, and then the grass and wildflowers took possession of the grave and hallowed it. Rude was the soil and lonely the spot—a rough rail enclosure, a surface stone to mark where lay the sleeper, or a cross of wood, or a name rudely cut upon the living bark of some adjacent tree, the sole memorial of the dead.

The lands have passed away from the families of the first breakers of the soil, and the peaceful dead are neglected in their lonely, unmarked resting places, forgotten by man, but not uncared for by Redeeming Love.

THE GRAVES OF THE EMIGRANTS

They sleep not where their fathers sleep,
    In the village churchyard's bound;
They rest not 'neath the ivied wall
    That shades that holy ground;

Nor where the solemn organ's peal
　　Pours music on the breeze,
Through the dim aisles at evening hour,
　　Or swells among the trees;

Nor where the turf is ever green,
　　And flowers are blooming fair
Upon the graves of the ancient men
　　Whose children rest not there;

Nor where the sound of warning bell
　　Floats mournfully on high,
And tells the tale of human woe,
　　That all who live must die.

Where, then, may rest those hardy sons
　　Who left their native shore
To seek a home in distant lands
　　Beyond the Atlantic's roar?

They sleep in many a lonely spot
　　Where mighty forests grow,
Where stately oak and lofty pine
　　Their darkling shadows throw.

The wild-bird pours her matin song
　　Above their lonely graves,
And far away in the stilly night
　　Is heard the voice of waves.

Fair lilies, nursed by weeping dews,
　　Unfold their blossoms pale,
And spotless snow-flowers lightly bend
　　Low to the passing gale.

The fire-fly lights her little spark
　　To cheer the leafy gloom,
Like Hope's blest ray that gilds the night
　　And darkness of the tomb.

Where moss-grown stone or simple cross
    Its silent record keeps,
There, deep within the forest shade,
    The lonely exile sleeps.[4]

INDIAN GRASS*[1]

⁂

This is one of the most remarkable of our native grasses, both as respects its appearance and habits as well as the use the Indian women make of it in the manufacture of all sorts of ornamental trifles and useful articles. They weave its long, flexible shining dark green leaves into baskets, mats, braids and many other things. As I write I have before me a cup and saucer neatly and skilfully woven together in one piece by the dusky fingers of an Indian squaw.

The Indian grass retains its color for a long time, and its fine aromatic perfume, resembling the scent of vanilla, remains for many years after it is cut and woven into the various articles made from it.

This grass, with the quills of the porcupine (which the squaws dye), moosehair, the bark of the silver or white birch and the inner bark of various other trees—bass, cedar, oak and beech—from which they make the coarser baskets, are the only stock-in-trade now left to the poor Indians.

The soil in which the Indian grass grows is for the most part light, sandy, low ground, near water, so the Indians tell me; but it is also found in

---

*The Indian Grass, commonly so-called, is the identical "Holy Grass" of northern Europe. The botanical name *Hierochloa* is derived from the Greek words meaning *sacred* and *grass*, the custom of strewing churches and other sacred buildings with this fragrant plant giving it the name. It was only when reading Smiles' "Memoirs of Robert Dick" (long after the above was written), and the account that naturalist gives of this plant, that I instantly recognized it as the same found in Ontario and used by the Indian women in their work.

prairie lands, where it is very beautiful, the husk or plume being of a purplish color and very bright and shining. Under cultivation it is very shy of blossoming, but the leaf attains to a great length. In my own garden it grows most luxuriantly, the blade often measuring nearly three feet.

It breaks the ground early in the spring, before any other grass has begun to show itself on the lawn. Like the spear grass it has a running root, pointed and sharp, to pierce the moist soil, and is hardy, remaining green and bright in cold or in summer drought. It does not give out its perfume until a few hours after it has been cut. One of its useful qualities lies in its toughness—it will not break when being twisted or braided, and can even be knotted or tied—and it is this elasticity which enables the Indian women to make it so available in their manufactures.

I have myself used it, making it into table mats, and find it pretty and useful for that purpose. I used to get from the Indians pretty braided chains, confined at intervals by bands or rings of dyed quills or beads. These I sent home to England, where they were highly esteemed for the work and the sweet scent of the grass. One of these chains is still in existence and has lost little of its fragrance.

I have sometimes suggested that the aroma might be utilized as a toilet article in the way of perfume.

The Indian women of the present generation are much more refined, and pay more attention to cleanliness in their habits that did their mothers and grandmothers. A lady who was returning to her friends in England asked me to procure for her some of these grass chains. I applied to an Indian woman, who readily set to work to supply them, seating herself under one of the trees in the grove near my garden. On going out to bring her refreshment, great was my dismay to see a great length of the grass braid wound round her by no means delicately clean big toe.

When I protested against this mode of proceeding, she laughed and said, "Good way, hold it all tight, nice."

But finding that I made great objection to her "nice way" of holding the braiding, she stuck a sharp stick into the ground, and fastened the coil of braid round it, and seemed convinced that this way was "nicer" than the other.

She had been perfectly unconscious that there was anything objectionable in her original mode of weaving the lady's chain until I pointed out its impropriety. Then she perceived it, and laughing, said, "Dirty foot, not nice."

The good-natured squaw took no offence with me for my disapproval of her primitive way of working. Gentle, patient, accustomed to be ruled from childhood, the Indian woman bears, suffers and submits without complaint.

Many a gentle Christian character have I known among the Indian women of the Rice Lake and Mud Lake villages, not unworthy of the name of the Master whose teachings they so meekly followed.

Indian Lodges on the Beach of the Island of Mackinac (Lake Huron, U.S.), 1837 by Anna Jameson.

The men die out, leaving widows and helpless children to be maintained. No one seems to care for the wants of the poor Indians beyond the officials whose part it is to carry out the regulations from the Indian Department of the Government in their behalf. But there seems to be a lack of sympathy shown to these poor people. They endure sickness and hunger, and suffer many trials in silence, never appealing for charity at any of the public institutions or private societies so long as they can work. The Indian will trade for bread, but rarely ever asks for it; he has a pride of his own, peculiar to his race.

He is not ungenerous by nature—indeed, an Indian loves to give little marks of his gratitude when kindly treated.

"Present for you," the squaw will say, laying beside your purchase a tiny canoe, a basket of birch bark, or some other trifle, and when money is offered in return she says, "*No, no, no*—for love of kindness to *me*."

There is something kindly in the Indian's nature. I like the words they close their letters with,

"I kiss you in my heart,
      From your Indian friend."

The Indian women outlive the men. Their quiet, peaceful temper, sobriety and industrious habits may account for this fact; but the men have not the same resources and are not in their natural state. Their spirit seems broken, and they become slow and inactive, and pine away early. Change of habit from the old out-of-door life of the hunter and trapper preying upon them, they die under the restrictive laws of civilization, and in another century it will be asked where is the remnant of the native race? and but that the dark eye, black hair and dusky skin may be traced in a few scattered individuals, it may be doubted if they ever existed or had left any descendants in the land.

MOSSES AND LICHENS

I FEAR my readers may turn over these few pages and regard the subjects as things of little worth—mosses and lichens, dry, uninteresting objects that we tread under our feet or pass by without giving them a second glance—and place them among the rough "Pebbles," not the choice "Pearls" of my collection.

Uninviting and trivial as the subject may be to many, I am confident that to the true lover of Nature they will not be without their interest, and may possibly direct attention to a world of beauty which has hitherto escaped his notice.

The lichens, the fungi and the mosses were probably the earliest forms of vegetable life. Before the grasses and small herbs these may have been created as a promise of what should clothe the young earth with verdure. The seaweeds (*Algæ*) may, indeed, have preceded them, and we might call them, not inaptly, the mosses of the seas, and place them at the head (as they are by right of priority) of the world of vegetation.

The most attractive of our mosses grow in the shadiest, thickest of our woods, where, at the foot of some huge maple, ash or elm, in the rich damp vegetable mould, you will find one of the handsomest and largest, the *Hypnum splendens*; or, it may be, forming a miniature forest on the decaying trunk of one of the prostrate giants of the wood, where it spreads its feathery fan-shaped fronds, branchlets which spring from a somewhat stiff and wiry stem, each set apparently denoting the product of a year's growth.

The foliage of these fan-shaped fronds is soft, much divided, and fringed with minute silky hairs. The older plants are of a darker hue, with a purplish shade in the centre. This adds much to the beauty of its appearance, and serves to distinguish this fine moss from the other species.

The *Hypnum splendens* is, I think, of perennial growth, as many specimens show the decayed fronds of former years. I have counted as many as nine on the same stem, besides the fresh green ones.

The capsules containing the sporules or seed appear on long slender stems, not more than two at the base of each of the fronds. This moss extends by roots as well as by the seed.

The wood moss (*Hypnum trignetram*) is coarser and more bushy, and though more striking in appearance, is not wanting in the peculiar grace of outline which is so attractive in the *Hypnum splendens*.

It is somewhat remarkable that the larger and more conspicuous plants of the moss tribe are less distinguished by their fruitage than the smaller ones, some of which, lowly, tiny, insignificant as to size, attract the eye by the bright array of shining capsules displaying the rich tints of red and brown, fawn or orange color. Very lovely these tiny cups look contrasted with the various shades of green, pale straw color, deep purplish-bronze, grey, silvery-white, or whatever the prevailing color of the moss may be.

There seems to be no end to the number and variety of species of mosses that are to be found, whether in the deep shade of the primeval forest, in swampy fens or bogs, in the water, floating and waving as the wind moves the surface, in the crevices of rocks where a little soil sustains them, or on the rugged stone which they clothe, as if to kindly hide the rough, bare surface.

No soil so barren, no desert so dry, but some kind of moss will find a spot where it may grow and flourish, take root and display its tufts of verdure, its rosy stems and capsules.

Look at this forest of red stalks, each crowned with a shining cap. The leaf is so minute you can hardly distinguish it, but the fruit is bright and beautiful. The soil is hard and arid, incapable of supporting anything save this Red Moss (*Ceratodon purpureus*).

"It drinks heaven's dew as blithe as rose
That in the King's own garden grows."[1]

It has indeed a great capacity for moisture, rain, snow and dew, which
appears to be the only food of the mosses that grow on desert lands. There
is the tiny *Bryum argenteum*, and others of the same genus, which take
possession of the least inviting soil, slate roofs, dry thatch, sapless wood
and hard clay banks where nothing else will grow.

All the species of this family are not so small. Some are conspicuous
for their fine coloring, such as the *Bryum roseum*, one not uncommonly
met with in the forest. Clusters of these may be found deeply nested in
old decayed logs among a variety of *Hypnums* and *Dicranums*. Their deep
green leafy rosettes, in shape like miniature roses, form a decided contrast to the sister mosses and grey lichens, and if it chance to be the fruit-
ing season, there is an added charm in the varied colors; for rising from
the cap-like centre of the crown of the plant are from three to five hair-
like stems about an inch in height, of a reddish color, almost semi-transparent, bearing a capsule blunt on the apex and a little curved downward
at the neck. This cap is orange-red, and looks as if it were a chalice filled
to the brim with some choice wine or amber-tinted fluid.

This curious vessel is closely sealed by a lid which, when the contents
are ripe, is lifted and the fine seed or sporules are poured out. This fruitful *Bryum* is sexsile, grows close to the ground, and extends largely by
means of its root-stalk, which sends up many shoots, each bud forming a
little leafy deep green cup.

A singularly handsome, tree-like variety is the Palm Tree Moss (*Cli-
macium Americanum*), but it is not a member of the *Bryum* family, being
distinct from it both in habit and appearance.

The appropriate name of Palm Tree Moss is derived from its plumy
head; the stem is often more than an inch high, bearing on its summit a
drooping crown of elegant feathery fronds, from the midst of which ascend
slender thready stalks bearing the long cylindrical pale red capsules.

When growing in the rich damp soil of the shady woods the full-grown
specimens are bright green, but in wet spongy places, exposed to the rays
of the sun, the plants take a bronze color, are stunted and thickset, and
have not the graceful appearance of those nurtured in the forest.

One of the most elegant of the somewhat stiffly growing mosses is the *Dicranum secundum*, which is of a slenderer habit than the *Dicranum scoparium*. In it the hair-like leafage is more scattered and borne on one side only. There are many species, and they are to be found in many places: some in damp woodlands, on logs, or on the ground; some on gneiss rocks and hillsides, forming thick level beds of velvety green, very bright and lovely, the dark capsules giving a fringe-like grace to the moss, relieving its uniformity and adding to the general effect.

On bare rugged rocks, dead wood and barren soil, a patch of silvery brightness catches the eye, and involuntarily we stop a moment to inspect one of the hardy little mosses of the wayside, the *Bryum argenteum*. It is so named from its silvery sheen, the brightness of its tiny capsules and the minuteness of its very inconspicuous foliage. It is the very least of the *Bryums*, yet the most fruitful; the little silvery caps are so close together that they form a shining host, and many a rugged spot is adorned and made attractive by them.

Perhaps it was some such insignificant moss as our *Bryum argenteum* that brought strength and comfort to the weary heart of the lonely African missionary, Mungo Park. Alone in the desert, despairing of all human aid, he had sunk down, and like the Hebrew prophet of old was ready to cry out, "It is better to die, than to live!" when his eye chanced to rest upon a little plant beside him, and attracted by its beauty, he argued thus within himself: "If the great Creator has thus preserved and nourished this little plant with the dew from heaven, and protected its helpless form so frail from injury, will He not also care for one for whom Christ died?" and rising from the arid desert he once more pursued his journey, strengthened by the sight of that simple desert plant.[2]

When these hardy little *Hypnums* and *Bryums* decay, they leave to their successors a sandy soil, part of which has been won from the hard rock on which they had found an abiding-place, their tiny, wedge-like roots having forced apart the surface of the limestone or gneiss rock, taking to themselves minute particles of the sterner material, thus forcing its strength to yield to their weakness. This is another proof of the wisdom of the Almighty God, who "willeth the weak things of the world and those that have no power to overcome the strong, and the base things of the world and the things that are despised hath He chosen to bring to nought things that are."[3]

Look now at this beautiful Feather Moss (*Hypnum tamariscinum*). Each frond is like a green plume, hence its descriptive name. Like *Hypnum splendens* it seems to be perennial, as may be inferred from the rather wiry stem bearing many divisions in the form of branchlets.

The plants of the first year's growth are single fronds, not branched, and it is the older and more matured that bear the long slender fruit-stalk and fine capsules containing the seed. There are seldom more than two to each of the lower pairs of leafy divisions. This species increases more by roots than by seed, as is the case with many of the larger mosses, and retains its color well when pressed and mounted in the herbarium.

I consider the most satisfactory method of preserving the mosses is to wash them thoroughly, no matter how you do it—squeeze them well (they are very elastic and come all right however roughly you handle them); then pick out such pieces as you wish to preserve, press the moisture from them with rag or blotting paper, old towel or any soft thing of the kind, and when pretty well dried, with a small brush and a little paste arrange them in a blank book or album of good stout paper. Always obtain the seed vessels, if possible, as it is by this particular organ of fructification that the family and different species are recognized.

A well-arranged book of mosses becomes a charming thing to inspect, and if the collector is fortunate in having a friend who is a botanist and who will help him to name his specimens, he will have a treasure book of very lovely objects to remind him of pleasant times spent in forest, swamp or field—a memento of wayside wanderings of days gone by, when the discovery of some new plant or moss or lichen was a source of pure and innocent delight, unalloyed by the experiences and cares of afterlife among his fellowmen in the hurry and strife of the busy world.

THE INDIAN MOSS BAG

BESIDES the use which is made of the white peat moss by the nurserymen and the gardeners, there is one which I will describe, as it will be new to those of my readers who are not acquainted with the interior of the Northwest Indians' wigwams, and the way the Indian mothers nurse and care for their babies.

The Indian moss bag takes the place of the cot or cradle—I might add, of the rocking chair, also, so indispensable in our nurseries. It is simply formed of a piece of cloth, or more usually of dressed doe skin, about two feet in length, shaped wider at the upper part and narrower below. The sides are pierced with holes in order that they may be laced together with a leather thong. On this skin is laid a soft bed of the dried moss, and the papoose (the Indian name for baby) is placed upon it, its hands and arms carefully disposed at its sides and the little legs and feet straight down and wrapped in a bit of fur, so that the tiny toes can feel no cold. The end of the bag is then folded over at the other end, turned up and the sides laced together. Nothing of baby is seen but its face and head. The black head and bead-like black eyes look very funny peering out of the moss bag. I forgot to mention that care is taken to support the back of baby's head by a pillow of the moss, the back portion of the bag being left a little higher than the front for that purpose.

A strong loop of braided bark or of finely-cut strips of doe skin is

attached to the moss bag, by which the primitive cradle may be suspended to the branch of a tree or to a peg in the wall of the lodge or house, or
be passed over the mother's forehead when travelling or moving from
place to place with the child on her back.

The infant seems perfectly at ease and contented. Of course, it is
released at times during the day and allowed to stretch its limbs on its
mother's lap or on the floor of the lodge, where a blanket or skin of some
wild animal is spread for it to lie upon.

Mississauga Indians in Canada, by Basil Hall, in *Forty Etchings, from Sketches Made
with the Camera Lucida, in North America, in 1827 and 1828* (1829).

So accustomed are the children to this original cradle bed that when
able to creep they will voluntarily seek for it and dispose themselves to
sleep, fretting if debarred from being put to rest in it.

Not only is this papoose cradle in use among the Indians, but in the
nurseries of the white settlers as well, and great taste and skill is shown
in the material of which they are made. Beautiful patterns in needlework
are wrought with silk, moose hair and beads by the ladies of the Hudson's
Bay Company to ornament their moss bags.

When older, the arms of the children are allowed to be free, and great
care is taken to keep the little ones bright and happy.

The Northwest papoose cradles are much better than those of our Ontario Indians, which are generally made of thin board or bark, while any sort of rags or blanket forms the bed for the babe. The squaw, when entering a house, will just slip the loop from her head and stick the cradle up against the wall, with very little care for the poor prisoner, who rarely cries, but peeps out from its shock of black hair perfectly contented to remain a silent spectator of the novelties by which it may be surrounded.

The mother often has a pad attached to the strap of the cradle, to prevent its sharp edges hurting her forehead when carrying the child in this way.

Now, it strikes me that our British ancestry may have been nursed in just such a fashion as that of the Northwest Indian moss bag. You know the old nursery lullaby song:

"Rock-a-by, baby, on the tree-top,
  When the wind blows the cradle will rock,
  When the bough breaks the cradle will fall,
  Then down comes cradle and baby and all."[1]

This ditty is as old as any of the ancient chronicles, handed down from age to age *verbatim* by nursing mothers of ancient days, a history in rhyme of how our ancestors were cradled.

SOMETHING GATHERS UP
THE FRAGMENTS

༄

"Something gathers up the fragments, and nothing is lost."
                            —*Fourcrois' Chemistry*[1]

THESE striking words, so suggestive of the wise economy[2] of the great Creator of the universe, are simply a paraphrase of the words of the Lord Jesus
given to His disciples after the miraculous feast of the hungry multitude
on the grassy slopes of Palestine, "Gather up the broken pieces which
remain over and above, that nothing be lost" (John vi. 13, Revised Ver-
sion)[3]—words which we are apt to read without entering fully into their
meaning.

We think only of their obvious import that no waste of provisions should
be allowed, that even the fragments should be gathered up and made use
of for ourselves or for the poor, but the old French chemist's eyes were
opened to see a wider and deeper meaning in the Lord's words.

He saw that in Nature, from the greatest to the smallest thing, there is no
waste. Unseen and unnoticed by us, every atom has its place and its part to
fulfil. Nothing is lost. In God's economy we trace this fact everywhere.

The waves of the mighty ocean are kept back by the atoms of sand worn
down from the lofty hills and rocks by the action of the winds and rains
and frosts of past ages. The minute particles are brought down by melted
snows of the avalanche to the rivers, and by the rivers to the seas. The

ocean waves bear these sands, mingled with their waters, to lay them softly down on the shore, there to form a barrier against their own encroach-
ments, unconsciously fulfilling the dictates of their mighty Creator's command, "Hitherto shalt thou come, but no further; and here shall thy proud
waves be stayed."[4]

Atom by atom were the lofty hills built up; atom by atom are they laid
low. By slow but constant action they perform the great work of keeping
back the advance of the mighty waves of the ocean and forming new land.

Chemistry presents many wonderful examples of the changes effected
by certain combinations known to the scientific searchers into the mysteries of Nature, but such things are out of the sphere of my limited
knowledge.

Let us rather go into the forests, where we may realize, not less forcibly,
the truth of the words, "Something gathers up the fragments, and nothing
is lost."

The depths of the forest present to the eye of the traveller a scene of
tangled confusion. Here fallen trees, with upturned roots, lie prostrate on
the ground; branchless, leafless, decaying trunks, unsightly to the eye;
beds of blackened leaves; shattered boughs, whitened and grey with fungus growth; naked stems ready to fall, their barkless wood graven with
many fantastic traceries, the work of the various insect larvae that have
sheltered therein their nurseries while the tree was yet living and strong.
A thousand forms of vegetable life are below, filling up the vacant places
of the soil.

In the silence of that lonely leafy wilderness there is active, sentient
life—nothing is idle, nothing stands still; instead of waste and confusion
we shall find all these things are working out the will of the Creator.

"Disorder—order unperceived by thee;
   All chance—direction which thou canst not see."[5]

Here lies one of the old giants of the forest at our feet. Take heed how
you step upon it. By its huge size and the pile of rifted bark beside it one
judges it must have had a growth of two hundred years, drinking in the
rain and the dews, and being fed by the gases that float unseen in the
atmosphere. The earth had sustained it year after year, giving strength and

support to the mighty trunk from its store of mineral substance through the network of cable-like roots and fibres. Never idle were those vegetable miners, always digging materials from the dark earth to add power and substance to the tree, hour by hour building up its wonderful structure, taking and selecting only such particles as were suited to increase the woody fibre and add to the particular qualities of the tree, whether it be oak, or ash, or maple, or the majestic pine.

But while the tree had been receiving, it had also year by year been giving back to earth and air, in an altered state, something that it did not require for itself. It had given back to the earth fresh matter, in the form of leaves, decayed branches and effete bark and fruitful seed. It had purified and changed the gases that it had first inhaled, and deprived them of the properties that were injurious to animal life. Something had gathered up the fragments that had been thrown off; there had been change, but not loss.

Now, let us look more closely at the surface of this fallen tree as it lies before us, a cumberer of the ground.

It is covered with variegated mosses, soft as piled velvet, but far more lovely. Here on the mouldering old wood are miniature forests, *Hypnums*, *Dicranums*, *Bryums*, with many lichens of the tenderest hues, grey, yellow or brown deepening to red, and, it may be, some brilliant fungus of gorgeous scarlet or cardinal red, fawn or gold, exquisite in form or in coloring, contrasting richly with the green of the mosses.

Possibly some reader will raise the question, Of what service can all these decaying trees and their coverings of mosses, lichens and fungi be to man? They have their uses, as we shall find if we examine the subject more closely, and notice the effects produced.

The floating germs of vegetable life, the seeds or spores of the lichens and mosses, falling on the surface of the fallen timber, find a soil suited to the peculiar requirements and development of their organisms. These minute vegetable growths are similar to those seen growing upon old rails and stumps and dry walls, and which anyone ignorant of their nature might think part of the substance to which they adhere, instead of living plants as the cryptograms all are. Simple plants, representing the earlier forms of vegetation in the world's history, worthy are they of reverence and adoration. These and others like them might be called the grey fathers of the vegetable kingdom.

As the lichens decay they give place to the mosses, and these, as they increase, send down their wedge-like roots between the fissures of the bark, penetrating into the tissue of the wood, already softened by the decomposition of the former occupants. The dew, the showers, the frosts and snows of winter, falling upon the sponge-like mosses, fill them with moisture, invigorate them and increase them till they form thick mats that hide the surface of the wood.

Some of these mosses, as we have seen, are not mere annuals, but, like the *Hypnum splendens* and other among the hair-cap mosses, are perennial.

Let us raise the thick mat of velvety mosses that are so minute and so closely packed. It presents a uniform smooth surface, and it seems a pity to disturb it in its beauty, but we would look beneath and see what its work has been during the past years.

A bed of rich black friable mould, the residue of the annual decomposition of these tiny mosses, meets the eye; below that mould we find layers of decaying wood, a loose network of fibrous matter. The cellular tissues have disappeared, and with the least pressure of hand or foot the whole fabric falls into a powdery mass.

The very heart of the wood has yielded up its strength and hardness under the influences of the agencies brought to bear upon it. A few more years and that fallen tree will be no more seen. The once mighty tree, with the mosses and lichens alike, will have returned their substance to Mother Earth. "Ashes to ashes, dust to dust."[6]

The little plants that penetrated to the heart of the vegetable giant of the woods have done their work, and are no more needed. The gases have been set free and restored to the atmosphere.

Let us sum up the work and see its results. The elements and the wood of the tree have fed the lichens and mosses. The mosses have been a warm sheltering home for myriads of insect larvae, which have gathered up many fragments during their infant state, all tending to reduce the wood to the earthy condition which should enter into other forms. Then comes man, a settler in the forest wilderness, a stranger and an emigrant from a far-off land. Coming to make himself a home, he must cut down the living trees and clear the ground with axe and fire. He sows the wheat and corn upon the rich black vegetable mould, but he may not think that he owes much of its fertility to the unseen, insignificant agents that for unnumbered ages, under the direction of the infinite God, have been preparing the ground to receive the grain for the life-sustaining bread for himself and his children.

Thus we see that by the heavenly Father's order, "Something gathers up the fragments, and nothing is lost."

"Whoso is wise, and will observe these things, even they shall understand the loving kindness of the Lord. " (Psa. cvii. 43)[7]

THE END

APPENDICES

INTRODUCTORY NOTE

MRS. TRAILL's book was already in the press when I was requested by the publisher to write a short biographical sketch of the author's life as an introduction.

Both time and space were limited, and I undertook the task with much anxiety, knowing that with such and other limitations I could scarcely expect to do the subject justice.

I have endeavored to use Mrs. Traill's own notes and extracts from her letters, wherever available, hoping thus to draw a life-like picture rather than enumerate the incidents of her life or put the records of the past into "cold type."

I have dwelt particularly on the circumstances of Mrs. Traill's childhood and youth, which I believe went far to influence her later life and direct her literary labors, and because they are also likely to be of greater interest to the public and the readers of her books than a mere detailed record of her life.

When asked some years ago by the editor of the *Young Canadians* to write a sketch of Mrs. Traill's life for its columns, the rider to the request was added that she "wished the sketch to be written with a loving pen—one that would depict the flowers rather than the thorns that had strewn her path," and I have in these few lines kept that kindly wish in view.

If I have failed to satisfy myself or others with my work, it has not been from lack of love for the honored and valued authoress of "*Pearls and Pebbles.*"

May we keep her long to bless us with her loving smile and happy, trustful spirit, and enrich our literature still further with the products of her graceful pen.

—*Mary Agnes FitzGibbon*

Toronto, December 4th, 1894.

BIOGRAPHICAL SKETCH

BY MARY AGNES FITZGIBBON (1894)

ALTHOUGH the family from which Catharine Parr Strickland (Mrs. Traill) is descended was one of considerable note and standing in the northern counties of England, her immediate ancestor was born and spent the greater part of his life in London.

The cause of the migration of this branch of the Strickland house was the unexpected return of Catharine's great-grandfather's elder and long-lost brother. He had been hidden at the Court of the exiled Stuarts, at St. Germains, and returned after an absence of upwards of twenty years, to claim the paternal estate of Finsthwaite Hall and its dependencies. He not only established his claim, but, with an ungenerous hand, grasped all the rents and revenues accruing to the property, and his nephew, then a student at Winchester College, disdaining to ask any favors of his uncle, left the now reduced comforts of Light Hall, his mother's jointure house, and went to seek his fortune in the metropolis. Being successful in the quest, he, after a time, married Elizabeth Cotterell, of the loyal Staffordshire family of that name, and maternally descended from one of the honest Penderel brothers, who protected Charles II in the oak at Boscobel, and succeeded, through their intrepid loyalty to the house of Stuart, in effecting his escape.

Of this marriage there were eight children: Thomas, born in 1758;

Samuel, in 1760, and two sisters. The remaining four fell victims to the smallpox, at that date an almost inevitably fatal disease.

Thomas, who was Catharine's father, early obtained employment with the ship-owners, Messrs. Hallet & Wells, and through them became master and sole manager of the Greenland docks, a position which threw him in the way of meeting many of the great men and explorers of the last century. He was twice married, first to a grand-niece of Sir Isaac Newton, and through her he came into possession of a number of books and other treasures formerly belonging to that celebrated scientist. Mrs. Strickland died within a few years of her marriage, having had only one child, a daughter, who died in infancy; and in 1793 Mr. Strickland married, as his second wife, Elizabeth Homer, who was destined to be the mother of a family of nine, five of whom have made a name in the literary annals of the century. Elizabeth and Agnes, afterward joint authoresses of "The Lives of the Queens of England," and each the writer of other historical biographies, poetry and other works; Sara and Jane, the latter author of "Rome, Regal and Republican," and other historical works, were born in London, Kent. There, also, on January 9th, 1802, Catharine Parr was born, and though named after the last queen of Henry VIII, who was a Strickland, she has always spelt her first name with a "C," and was ever known in the home circle by the more endearing words "the Katie."

Mr. Strickland's health being affected by too close application to business, he was advised to retire and take up his residence in the more bracing climate of the eastern counties.

After living a few months at "The Laurels," in Thorpe, near Norwich, he rented "Stowe House," an old place in the valley of the Waveney, not far from the town of Bungay.

"The first and happiest days of my life were spent at 'Stowe House,' in that loveliest of lovely valleys the Waveney," she writes; and truly there is no spot in all England that can vie with it in pastoral beauty.

The highroad between Norwich and London passes behind the site of the old house, separated and hidden from it by the high, close-cropped hedge and noble, wide-spreading oaks. The house (pulled down only within the last few years) stood on the slope of the hill, and below, at the foot of the old world gardens and meadow, the lovely river winds its silvery way to the sea. The green hills, the projecting headlands, the tiny hamlets clus-

tered about the ivy-covered church towers of fifteenth and sixteenth century architecture; the beauty of the velvety meadows and the hawthorn
hedges; the red-tiled cottages with their rose-clad porches, and beyond,
against the sky, the old grey towers and massive walls of that grand old
stronghold, the Castle of Bungay, where the fierce Earl Marshal of England had defied the might and menace of the "King of all Cockaynie and
all his braverie," altogether form a scene it would be difficult to equal in
any quarter of the globe.

Reydon Hall, from Pearls and Pebbles (1894).

Among other rooms in "Stowe House," there was a small brick-paved
parlor, which was given up entirely to the children. Here they learned
their lessons, waited in their white dresses for the footman to summon
them to the diningroom for dessert, or played when debarred by unpropi-
tious weather from the "little lane" so prettily described by Mrs. Traill in
"Pleasant Days of my Childhood."

Many anecdotes and stories have been told me by the elder sisters of
the hours spent within the oak-panelled walls and by the great fire-place
of the brick parlor, of the pranks and mischief hatched there against the
arbitrary rule of a trusted servant who hated the "Lunnon children" in
proportion as she loved the Suffolk-born daughters of the house. Here they
learned and acted scenes from Shakespeare, pored over great leather-

bound tomes of history, such as a folio edition of Rapin's "History of England," with Tyndall's notes, and printed in last century type. Here Agnes and Elizabeth repeated to the younger children Pope's "Homer's Iliad," learned out of Sir Isaac Newton's own copy, or told them stories from the old chronicles.

Mr. Strickland was a disciple of Isaak Walton and a devoted follower of the "gentle craft," but being a great sufferer from the gout, required close attendance. Katie generally accompanied him to the river, and though Lockwood, a manservant who had been with him many years, was always at hand, Katie could do much to help her father, and became very expert in handling his fishing tackle, while still a very small child. One of Mrs. Traill's most treasured possessions now is a copy of the first edition of "The Compleat Angler," which formerly belonged to her father.

When talking of her childhood, Sara (Mrs. Gwillym) always spoke of "the Katie" as the idolized pet of the household. "She was such a fair, soft blue-eyed little darling, always so smiling and happy, that we all adored her She never cried like other children—indeed we used to say that Katie never saw a sorrowful day—for if anything went wrong she just shut her eyes and the tears fell from under the long lashes and rolled down her cheeks like pearls into her lap. My father idolized her. From her earliest childhood she always sat at his right hand, and no matter how irritable or cross he might be with the others, or from the gout, to which he was a martyr, he never said a cross word to 'the Katie.' "

"Stowe House" was only a rented property, and when, in 1808, "Reydon Hall," near Wangford, fell into the market, Mr. Strickland bought it and removed his family to the new home at the end of the year.

"Well do I remember the move to Reydon that bitter Christmas Eve," said Mrs. Traill, when speaking of it on last Thanksgiving Day, her eyes shining as bright as a child's with the recollection. "The roads were deep in snow, and we children were sent over in an open tax-cart with the servants and carpenters. It was so cold they rolled me up in a velvet pelisse belonging to Eliza to keep me from freezing, but I was as merry as a cricket all the way, and kept them laughing over my childish sallies. We stopped at a place called 'Deadman's Grave' to have some straw put into the bottom of the cart to keep us warm. No, I shall never forget that journey to Reydon through the snow."

A fine old Elizabethan mansion, of which the title-deed dates back to the reign of Edward VI, "Reydon Hall" was a *beau ideal* residence for the bringing up of a family of such precious gifts as the Strickland sisters. It stands back from the road behind some of the finest oaks, chestnuts and ashes in the county. Built of dark brick, its ivy-covered wall, its gabled roof, tall chimneys, stone-paved kitchen, secret chambers and haunted garrets suited both their imaginative and fearless natures. A magnificent sycamore in the centre of the lawn, a dell at the end of "the plantation" (as a wide open semi-circular belt of oaks was called), and the beautiful Reydon Wood to the north, on the Earl of Stradbroke's property, formed a grand environment for the development of their several characteristics.

Mr. Strickland educated his elder daughters himself, and having a fine library, they were given an education far superior to that which generally fell to the lot of the daughters of that date. He had purchased a house in Norwich, and always spent some months of the year in that beautiful old cathedral city, and as the attacks of gout increased in frequency, was obliged to reside there during the winter. He was generally accompanied by one or two of his daughters, his wife dividing her time as much as possible between the two houses. During her absence from Reydon, the care and education of the younger children devolved upon their eldest sister Elizabeth.

That the literary bent showed itself early will be seen by the following account, which I cannot refrain from giving as much in Mrs. Traill's own words as possible:

"We passed our days in the lonely old house in sewing, walking in the lanes, sometimes going to see the sick and carry food or little comforts to the cottagers; but reading was our chief resource. We ransacked the library for books, we dipped into old magazines of the last century, such as Christopher North styles 'bottled dulness in an ancient bin,' and dull enough much of their contents proved. We tried history, the drama, voyages and travels, of which latter there was a huge folio. We even tried 'Locke on the Human Understanding.' We wanted to be very learned just then, but as you many imagine, we made small progress in that direction, and less in the wonderfully embellished old tome, 'Descartes' Philosophy.' We read Sir Francis Knolles' 'History of the Turks,' with its curious woodcuts and quaint old-style English. We dipped into old Anthony Horneck's book of 'Divine Morality,' but it was really *too* dry. We read Ward's 'History of the Reformation in Rhyme,' a book that had been condemned to be burnt by the common hangman. How this copy had escaped I never learned. I remember how it began:

> " 'I sing the deeds of good King Harry,
> And Ned his son and daughter Mary,
> And of a short-lived inter-reign
> Of one fair queen hight Lady Jane.'

"We turned to the *Astrologer's Magazine* and so frightened the cook and housemaid by reading aloud its horrible tales of witchcraft and apparitions that they were afraid to go about after dark lest they should meet the ghost of old Martin, an eccentric old bachelor brother of a late proprietor of the Hall, who had lived the last twenty years of his life secluded in the old garret which still bore his name and was said to be haunted by his unlaid spirit. This garret was a quaint old place, closeted round and papered with almanacs bearing dates in the middle of the past century. We children used to puzzle over the mystical signs of the Zodiac, and try to comprehend the wonderful and mysterious predictions printed on the old yellow paper. There was, too, a tiny iron grate with thin rusted bars, and the hooks that had held up the hangings of the forlorn recluse's bed. On one of the panes in the dormer windows there was a rhyme written with a diamond ring, and possibly of his own composition:

> " 'In a cottage we will live,
> Happy, though of low estate,
> Every hour more bliss will bring,
> We in goodness shall be great.—M.E.'

"We knew little of his history but what the old servants told us. He had never associated with the family when alive. His brother's wife made him live in the garret because she disliked him, and he seldom went abroad. All the noises made by rats or the wind in that part of the house were attributed to the wanderings of poor Martin. There was also a little old woman in grey, who was said to 'walk' and to play such fantastic tricks as were sufficient to turn white the hair of those she visited in the small hours of the night.

"Had we lived in the days of 'spiritualism' we should have been firm believers in its mysteries. The old Hall with its desolate garrets, darkened windows, worm-eaten floors, closed-up staircase and secret recesses might have harbored a legion of ghosts—and as for rappings, we heard plenty of them. The maidservants, who slept on the upper floor, where stood the huge mangle in its oaken frame (it took the strong arm of the gardener to turn the crank), declared that it worked by itself, the great linen rollers being turned without hands unless it were by those of ghosts. No doubt the restless little woman in grey had been a notable housewife in her time, and could not remain idle even after being in her grave for a century or more.

"To relieve the tedium of the dull winter days, Susan and I formed the brilliant notion of writing a novel and amusing ourselves by reading aloud at night what had been written during the day. But where should we find paper? We had no pocket-money, and even if we had been amply supplied there was no place within our reach where we could purchase the means of carrying out our literary ambitions. Enthusiastic genius is not easily daunted, and fortune favored us. In the best room there was a great Indian *papier-mache* chest with massive brass hinges and locks. It had contained the wardrobe of a young Indian prince who had been sent to England with an embassy to the Court of one of the Georges. This chest was large enough to fill the space between the two windows, and hold the large rosewood and bamboo cot with its hangings of stiff cream-white brocaded silk embroidered with bunches of roses, the colors still brilliant and unfaded, alternating with strips worked in gold and silver thread. The four curtains of this luxuriant tented cot were looped with thick green ribbons. There were ancient damasks, silks, old court dresses that had belonged to some *grande dame* of Queen Anne's reign, and turbans of the finest India muslin of great length and breadth, yet of so fine a texture that the whole width of one could be drawn through a lady's finger ring. My mother had also made the old chest a receptacle for extra stores of house-linen, and underneath all she had deposited may reams of paper, blotting paper, and dozens of ready-cut quill pens which had been sent to our father on the death of his brother, who had been a clerk in the Bank of England.

Here was treasure trove. We pounced on the paper and pens—their being cut adding much to their value—and from some cakes of Indian ink we contrived to manufacture respectable writing fluid. Among the old books in the library there was a fine atlas in two quarto volumes, full of maps and abounding in the most interesting geographical histories of the European countries, legends, the truth of which we never questioned, and flourishing descriptions that just suited our romantic ideas of places we had never seen but had no difficulty in picturing to ourselves. I chose the period of my hero William Tell, intending to write an interesting love tale; but I soon got my hero and heroine into an inextricable muddle, so fell out of love adventures altogether, and altering my plan ended by writing a juvenile tale, which I brought to a more satisfactory conclusion. Every day we wrote a portion, and at night read it aloud to Sara. She took a lively interest in our stories and gave us her opinion and advice, of which we took advantage to improve them the following day. Not feeling quite sure of our mother's approval, we kept our manuscripts carefully concealed after her return, but we were in even greater dread of our eldest sister, knowing that she would lecture us on the waste of time.

"One morning I was sitting on the step inside our dressing-room door, reading the last pages of my story to Sara, when the door behind me opened and a small white hand was quietly placed on mine and the papers extracted. I looked at Sara in dismay. Not a word had been spoken, but I knew my mother's hand, and the dread of Eliza's criticism became an instant reality; and her 'I think you had been better employed in improving your grammar and spelling than in scribbling such trash,' sounded cruelly sarcastic to my sensitive ears. I, however, begged the restoration of the despised manuscript, and obtained it under promise to curl my hair with it.

"I did in truth tear up the first part, but a lingering affection for that portion of it containing the story of the 'Swiss Herd-boy and his Alpine Marmot,' induced me to preserve it, and I have the rough copy of that story now in my possession."

Early in the spring of the following year, May 18th, 1818, Mr. Strickland died at Norwich. The sudden tidings of the failure of a firm in which he had allowed his name to remain as a sleeping partner or guarantor, and the consequent loss of the principal part of his private income, brought on an aggravated attack of the gout, which terminated fatally. Katie had spent the winter with him and her sisters Eliza and Agnes in the town house. Mrs. Strickland was at Reydon, but was to return the following day to prepare for the usual move to the old Hall for the summer.

Mr. Strickland's sudden death was a great shock to his family, and Katie grieved much for him. He had always been indulgent to her, and his loss was her first sorrow, the first cloud on her young life. Here I may quote again from her own notes:

"We had often heard our father express a wish to be buried in some quiet churchyard beyond the walls of the city, in the event of his death taking place before his return to Reydon, and in accordance with that wish he was laid to rest at Lakenham, a lovely rural spot about two miles from Norwich. There we three sisters, true mourners, often resorted during the summer evenings to visit the dear father's resting place, and bring a loving tribute of fresh flowers to strew upon the grave."

The house in Norwich was retained, and as the two brothers were attending Dr. Valpy's school, the two elder sisters and Katie remained there. Elizabeth, having been her father's amanuensis and confidante, had much to do in connection with business matters. Agnes was not strong, and requiring frequent change of air, was much away visiting friends. Katie was thus left very much to herself.

"I had access to the city library, so that I had no lack of reading matter, and my needle, varied by a daily walk to the garden below the city wall, occupied a good deal of my time. The garden was shut in by a high paling and was quite private. I spent many hours in this retreat with my books, and it was at this time that I ventured once more to indulge the scribbling fever which had been nipped in the bud by adverse criticism the proceeding year. I was a great lover of the picturesque, and used to watch with intense interest the Highland drovers as they passed to the great Norwich market. I admired their blue bonnets and the shepherd's plaids they wore so gracefully across breast and shoulder, and the rough coats of the collie dogs that always accompanied them, and often listened to the wild notes of the bagpipes. Scotland was the dream of my youth. Its history and poetry had taken a strong hold on my fancy, and I called the first story I wrote at this time, 'The Blind Highland Piper.' The next was inspired by a pretty little lad with an earnest face and bright golden curls peeping from under a ragged cap. He carried a wooden yoke on his shoulders, from which were suspended two water pails. He passed the window so often to and fro that I grew to watch for him, and give him a little nod and smile to cheer his labors day by day. I never knew his history, so I just made one for him myself, and called my story after him, 'The Little Water-Carrier.' Thus I amused myself until my collection comprised some half-dozen tales. One day I was longer than usual absent at the city wall garden gathering red currants, and had unwittingly left my manuscript on the writing-table. On my return, to my confusion and dismay, I found it had been removed. I could not summon courage to question my sister about it, so said nothing of my loss. A few days passed, and I began to fear it had been burned, but on the next visit of our guardian, Mr. Morgan, on business connected with my father's estate, he said to my eldest sister, 'Eliza, I did not know that you had time for story writing,'

"My sister looked up in surprise and asked him what he meant. Taking my lost property out of his pocket he replied, 'I found this manuscript open on the table, and, looking over its pages, became at once interested and surprised at your work.'

"Eliza looked inquiringly at me, and though confused and half frightened, I was obliged to claim the papers as mine.

"Our kind friend then added as he rolled up the manuscript and replaced it in his pocket, 'Well, Katie, I am going to correct this for you,' and I, glad to escape without a rebuke for waste of time or indulging in such idle fancies, thought no more of my stories. A month afterwards Mr. Morgan, with a smiling face, put into my hands five golden guineas, the price paid for my story by Harris the Publisher, in St. Paul's Churchyard, London."

Thus was Mrs. Traill the first of the Strickland sisters to enter the ranks of literature, as she is now the last survivor of that talented *coterie*. The unexpected success of Katie's first venture no doubt induced her sisters to send their MSS to the publishers. How their work has been recognized is matter of history.

"The Blind Highland Piper, and Other Tales" was so well received by the public that Katie was employed by Harris to write another for his House. "Nursery Tales" proved a greater success, although the remuneration she received was not increased. She next wrote for the Quaker House of Messrs. Darton & Harvey, "Prejudice Reproved," "The Young Emigrants," "Sketches from Nature," "Sketch Book of a Young Naturalist," and "The Stepbrothers." This firm paid her more liberally than Harris, and it was with the utmost delight and pleasure that she sent the proceeds of her pen to her mother at Reydon, grateful that she was able to help even in so small a way to eke out the now reduced income of the home.

Messrs. Dean & Mundy published "Little Downy, the Field-mouse," and "Keepsake Guinea, and Other Stories," in 1822. Many other short stories were written and published in the various Annuals issued between that year and Katie's marriage in 1832. "Little Downy, the Field-mouse" was the most popular, and is, I believe, still in print. None of the early works of the sisters were written over their own names, and a late edition of this story was issued by the publishers over Susanna's (Mrs. Moodie) name, and though both the sisters wrote protesting against the blunder and requesting a correction, no notice was taken of their letters.

"Little Downy was a real mouse," said Mrs. Traill recently, when speaking of her early works, "and I well remember how I wrote its story. I used to sit under the great oak tree near where it lived, and watch the pretty creature's frisky, frolicing ways, and write about it on my slate. When I had both sides covered I ran into the house and transcribed what I had written in an old copybook, then ran out again to watch the gentle dear and write some more."

During the years which intervened between the death of her father and her marriage, nothing of very great moment occurred in Katie's life, save the falling in of a small legacy as her share of a deceased uncle's property. She made occasional visits to London, where she stayed with a cousin of her father's or with other friends—visits full of interest from the people she met, the glimpses obtained of fashionable life, and the often amusing adventures which ever fall to the lot of those who go about the world with their eyes open. Katie's brilliant complexion, soft beauty and sunny smile won her the love and admiration of all with whom she came in contact, and she was always a welcome guest with old and young alike.

The means at Reydon were narrow, and in those days poverty was regarded almost as a crime, so they lived quietly in the old Hall, sufficient society for each other, and each pursuing the line of study in accordance with the particular bent of her individual genius.

Susanna had married in 1831, and came with her husband* to live at Southwold, and it was at their house that Katie met her future husband. Mr. Thomas Traill belonged to one of the oldest families in Orkney. He was also a friend and brother officer of Mr. Moodie's in the 21st Royal Scotch Fusiliers, and the two families of Moodie and Traill had been connected by marriage in more than one generation. Educated at Baliol College, Oxford, in the same year with Lockhart, who was an intimate friend, Mr. Traill could number many of the great writers and men of the day among his acquaintances, and knew many anecdotes of Scott, Giffard, Jeffreys and Wilson. He had married first an Orkney lady, and her health requiring a warner climate, he had lived abroad for several years and enjoyed the opportunity of meeting some of the great men of literature and science at the courts of Paris and Berlin. He was an excellent linguist and a well-read man.

At the time of his visit to Southwold his wife had been dead some years, his two sons were in Orkney with their mother's relatives, and he, having no settled plan for the future, was ready to take a lively interest in the question of emigration to Canada, the new country at that time being widely advertised and lectured upon, and in which free grants of land were being offered as an inducement to retired and half-pay officers to try their fortunes in the New World.

Katie met him at her sister's house, and it was not very long before it became known to the family at Reydon that Mr. Traill meant to precede the Moodies to Canada—and that he was not to go alone.

The grief of the sisters was great at the idea of parting with the beloved Katie. At first they refused to believe so preposterous a tale, but "the Katie" had made her choice and no entreaties could prevail upon her to change her mind. They were married on May 13th, 1832, in the parish church at Reydon, by the vicar, the Reverend H. Birch. It was a very quiet wedding, and a sad one, for the shadow of the coming parting was over them all.

"On the 20th of May I bade farewell to my old home and the beloved mother whom I was never again to see on earth, and, accompanied by my sisters Agnes and Jane, went down to the beach, from whence we were to

---

*John W. D. Moodie (youngest son of Moodie of Melsetter, Orkney), late Lieut. 21st Fusiliers, and author of "Ten Years in South Africa," "A Soldier and Settler," etc.

be rowed out to embark on the *City of London*, one of the first two steamers which then plied between the metropolis and Leith.

"It was a Sunday and a lovely bright morning, the heavens cloudlessly blue and the sea without a ripple save that of the incoming tide; the waves running in in curving lines along the beach, with a murmuring music all their own. The bells from the tower of the grand old church of St. Edmund were chiming their summons to the morning service, but they seemed to me to be repeating the sad refrain—

"   'Parting forever,
Parting forever,
Never again to meet!
   Never, O never!'

Yet as I leaned over the side of the ship and watched the boat that conveyed my sisters back to the shore until it was a mere speck upon the ocean, I little dreamed that my eyes should never again look upon those dear ones and England's loved shores. Hope was ever bright. To me there was always a silver lining to every cloud, and surely it is a gift of God that it has ever been so, that in the darkest hours of the sorrows, privations and troubles of after years I could look up and say, 'Thy will be done.'"

After a stay of two or three days in Edinburgh, the Traills embarked in the old *Pomona* packet for Kirkwall.

Mrs. Traill was received by her husband's relations and by his first wife's sisters and father with the utmost kindness and affection, although no one could have appeared in worse plight to captivate unknown relatives than she did that morning, wet from the sea spray, weary and weak from the effects of the stormy passage. One of these sisters, Miss Fotheringham[e], is still living in London at the advanced age of ninety-one, and I have sat beside the beautiful white-haired old lady and listened with delight to her description of the arrival of the English bride their brother-in-law brought so unexpectedly to their house at Kirkwall.

"We were not altogether pleased at the tidings of his marriage, but we fell in love with his second wife before she had been a day in the house; and truly she was a lovely, bright sunny creature to take out to the untracked wilds of a colony."

After a stay of some weeks in the Islands, they returned to Scotland to sail from the Clyde in the last vessel of the season bound for Quebec and Montreal.

The following word-picture of the parting at Kirkwall is descriptive of the tenacious affection felt by the tenantry and dependents for their feudal lairds, who hold rank and titles peculiar to the islands, and which are derived from their descent from the Norse Vikings who in former ages so often defied the power of the Scottish kings:

"Assembled on the Kirkwall pier, we found about twenty-five of the Westove tenantry. They had come down to take leave of their old master. Among them was auld Jean Scott, the nurse or *moome* of my husband. He, wishing to propitiate her in my favor, had provided me with a handful of coins to give her. Though her hand closed over the silver, she continued to regard me with a stern and forbidding countenance,—I was a stranger and a foreign body, not one of their island folk. In wild, impassioned tones she entreated the master to stay in his 'ain countrie an' amang his ain people and kin.' Then turning to me she said angrily, 'An' it is ye that are takin' him awa' frae us. Ye are bonnie eneuch, an' if ye wad but speak the word he maunna deny ye; but ye wauna, ye wauna dae it,' and flinging back my hand she threw herself on her knees at her master's feet, sobbing out, 'Ye will gae awa, an' these e'en that see ye the noo wull see ye nae mair.'

"My husband lifted and tried to soothe her, but she would not be comforted. Ah, Jean! you spoke truly; the master you so loved and honored lies in the little churchyard on the banks of the Otonabee, far from the Lady Kirk of his Orkney Island home."

At Inverness, Mrs. Traill first saw a Highland regiment "all plaided and plumed in their tartan array," and heard the pipes playing the grand Highland "March of the Cameron Men." Her enthusiasm, as well as her intimate knowledge of the Scottish writers, won her golden opinions and the English bride received much attention from the Highland descendants of the men who had striven to the death for the cause of the Stuarts.

"I was far from quite well when we left Inverness by the little passenger steamer *Highland Chieftain*, yet not too ill to find myself, in company with others of the passengers, climbing the steep winding path which led from the waters of Loch Ness to the Falls of Foyers and plucking many sweet wildflowers by the way. My love for flowers attracted the attention of two of my companions, a Mr. Allen, of Leith, and a Mr. Sterling, of Glasgow, both of whom I found were horticulturalists and well acquainted with the *flora* of the country. We entered into conversation, and they added much to the pleasure of the journey by pointing out to me the interesting objects along our route. At Glen Morrison, a fine old gentleman with his fishing basket and tackle was rowed out to the boat by two barefooted Highland lassies, stout girls who plied the oars with as powerful a stroke as any of the fisher lads of Cromarty. I must have eyed the fishing basket with a longing glance (it reminded me of my childhood days on the bank of the Waveney), for the old laird noticed me and we became quite friendly. He talked of salmon fishing and Highland lochs, and pointed out the wild opening of Lochiel's Glen. Then we spoke of the Camerons and the Macdonells, the Stewarts and Glencoe, the Highland chiefs and Highland feuds and emigration, and I told him we were bound for the far west. Before he left the boat at a point leading to Inverary, he held my hand a few seconds and said: 'If you should ever be near the Highland settlement of Glengarry, and need help or shelter, say that you have seen *the Macdonell*, and every door will be opened to you, every Highland hand held out in token of friendship.'

"That night we spent in a clean little public house within sight of the giant Ben Ness, the hostess of which talked much of Sir Walter Scott, whom she had known well. The illness I had felt coming on when in Inverness was only stayed, and it now overtook me, robbing me of all the pleasure of the lovely scenery of the Clyde, and by the time we reached Greenock I was completely prostrated. Skillful treatment and careful nursing, however, enabled me to recover sufficiently to be carried on board the brig *Laurel*, in which our passage had been taken and paid for, and which it would have been a serious loss to forfeit."

Mrs. Traill speaks of this brig as being the last of the season sailing from that port to Quebec. They sailed on the 7th of July, a fact and date which bear interesting comparison with the carrying trade of the present time between the Clyde and Canada.

The passage was a good one, unbroken by storms or fogs, and although very ill during the first part of the voyage, by the time the *Laurel* entered the Gulf, Mrs. Traill had quite recovered her health. The trip up the river was a slow one; there was little wind, and they had to depend largely on the tide for their onward progress, tacking constantly to take advantage of what breeze there was, and casting anchor when the tide turned. They were also delayed waiting for a pilot, and did not reach Quebec until late on the evening of August 15th, and on the 17th cast anchor before Montreal.

The Traills went to the Nelson Hotel until they could have their baggage passed through the Custom house, always a tedious business, and particularly so at that date. The weather was intensely hot. Cholera was raging in the city, and before the two days of delay had expired Mrs. Traill was stricken down with the terrible disease. She was tenderly cared for by a woman in the inn, a sister of the proprietor, to whose fearless devotion, as well as to the skilful treatment of Dr. Caldwell, she owed her recovery. Worn out by his untiring efforts among the cholera patients, this devoted physician fell a victim to the disease about a month later.

Although narrowly escaping death, the recuperative vitality which has ever been the characteristic feature of the family, enabled her to recover quickly, and on the 29th, Mrs. Traill was sufficiently recovered to health to continue her journey by stage to Lachine, and thence by boat and stage to Prescott, where they took their passage on board the *Great Britain*, then the largest and best steamer on the route.

In the sketch, "Sunset and Sunrise on Lake Ontario," Mrs. Traill gives an account of the journey from Brockville to Cobourg. On September 9th, they left Cobourg in a light waggon for the shores of Rice Lake, there to take the steamer for Peterborough, in the neighborhood of which place Mrs. Traill's brother, who had emigrated to Canada some years before, had lately settled.

"A motley group of emigrants shared the only available room in the log house which did duty as tavern on the shores of Rice Lake. The house consisted of but two rooms, the kitchen and one other apartment or public room. In a corner, on a buffalo robe spread on the floor, and wrapped in my Scotch plaid cloak, I rested my weary limbs. The broad rays of the full moon, streaming in through the panes of the small window, revealed our companions of the Cobourg stage, talking, smoking, or stretched at full length sleeping. On a rude couch at the other end of the room lay a poor sick woman, tossing and turing in a state of feverish unrest, moaning or muttering her delirious fancies, unconscious of the surroundings.

"Our early six o'clock breakfast of fried pork, potatoes, and strong tea without milk, was not very tempting, and it was but a scant portion of the rude meal that I could take. Leaving the crowded table, we strolled down to the landing place, where a large party of Irish emigrants were encamped. It was a curious scene. What studies of the picturesque for a painter were there! Men in all sorts of ragged coats and brimless hats and huge wrinkled brogues; women with red handkerchiefs tied over their dishevelled locks, and wearing jackets that had once done duty as part of a regimental uniform. There was many a pretty foot coquettishly peeping from beneath a quilted petticoat to be hastily hidden by the black-eyed owner, when she noticed the stranger's approach. A smart young fellow, hat in hand, came forward to know if the 'jintleman' would like to see an Irish jig or a 'toe the plank'—a feat which was performed by two men dancing a wild sort of horn-pipe with a wonderful variety of turnings and twistings, capers and wrestlings, as trials of skill and strength, on a board or door laid on the ground, until one was forced to yield and lose his balance. Of course a reward was expected, though not asked, and a cheer given for the 'jintleman' by the actors and spectators. An empty flask then made its rounds for the whiskey that was not in it, but hoped for. One old crone noticed my husband's foreign habit of taking snuff, and hobbling up to him presented her own snuff box, with a significant tap to show that it was empty. It was a tiny receptacle and was replenished at once, to her infinite satisfaction. Among the older women there were many sad and anxious faces, while the younger ones were bright and evidently hopeful for the future. Two nice-looking girls interested me, they were so neat and quiet in comparison with the others. One had a piece of very beautiful work in her hand, which she hastily concealed in the bosom of her dress. 'It is only a bit of our Irish lace,' she said, in answer to my inquiry, 'and it is not nice, it is not clean!' Poor thing, how could she keep her thread and pretty work clean amid such surroundings?

"The little steamer *Pem-o-dash*, the Indian word for 'fire-boat,' which was to convey us across the lake and up the river to Peterborough, had no cabin, was half-decked, and carried a sail in addition to the steam propeller. When she stopped to take in a supply of wood at a clearing about half way, I seized the opportunity to land and gather some of the splendid cardinal flowers that grew along the shores. Here, too, I plucked as sweet a rose as ever graced an English garden. There was also a bush resembling our hawthorn, which on examination I found to be the Cockspur hawthorn. It had fruit as large as cherries, pulpy and of a pleasant flavor, not unlike tamarind. The thorns were of great length and strength. Among the grasses of the meadow land I found spearmint, and, nearer to the bank, quantities of peppermint. Owing to the rapids and the shallowness of the river, the steamboat was unable to go up the whole way to Peterborough, so a large, unwieldly-looking scow had been engaged to meet it at a point called the 'Yankee Bonnet,' so named from a fanciful resemblance the topmost branches of a tree growing on the bank had to the sort of cap worn by the Yankees. The steamer, however, ran aground some four miles below the rendezvous. This caused a considerable delay and gave rise to much ill-humor among the boatmen at having to row down to meet the steamer. The boat was heavily laden, the men surly, and night had closed in before we heard the sound of the rapids ahead. The moon had now risen, and the stars were shining brilliantly over the water, which gave back the reflection of a glorious multitude of heavenly bodies. A sight so surpassingly beautiful might have stilled the most turbulent spirits, and I leaned back against my husband's supporting arm and looked from sky to star-lighted river, from the river up to the sky, with unspeakable delight and admiration. But my reverie was rudely broken by the grounding of the boat against the rocky bank, and the loud protests of the men against rowing another stroke or attempting the rapids that night. We were two miles distant from the town, the dark forest lay gloomy and dense before us, and I was weak from illness and want of food. To pass the night on an open scow, exposed to the heavy dews and chill air, would be death. It was ten o'clock, and the outlook was not encouraging. How were we to make our way through an unknown forest to the town?

"One of our fellow-passengers, whose house lay on the opposite bank of the river, and who had engaged one of the boatmen to put him across, yielded to Mr. Traill's entreaties to allow us to accompany him. Remaining only long enough at this settler's house to take a cup of tea, we procured the services of a little Irish lad and a lantern to guide us through the remaining bit of bush which still separated us from the town, and set forth on our travels to seek a shelter for the night. Our little Irish lad was very full of sympathy for the 'English leddy who looked so tired.' He told us of how he had lost both father and mother from cholera at Montreal, and was alone in the world without anyone to care for him. Our way was crossed by a little stream, over which the only bridge was the rough trunk of a fallen tree. The heavy dew had made it wet and slippery, and in crossing my head turned dizzy and I slipped, wetting my feet, thereby adding one more to my other discomforts. Beyond the stream the forest opened out into a wide grassy plain, and the lights from a few scattered houses told us we were on the site of the now populous city of Peterborough.

" 'Now, mistress, and yer honor,' said our little guide, 'here is the Government House, an' I cannot show ye any furder bekase I don't know any of the town beyant, but I'll call up Mr. Roseberry, an' shure he'll guide ye to the hotel.'

"Mr. Roseberry's man obeyed the summons, and appearing in a wonderful *deshabille*, directed us to Mr. McFadden's hotel, which, if not shut up, would afford us a night's lodging. Hurrying down the steep hill we found the house still open, but only to learn that there was no room, every available space being occupied by a recent influx of newly-arrived emigrants. This seemed the crowning misfortune to a disastrous day. We inquired how far we were from Mr. Stewart's—friends to whom we had brought letters from Montreal—and were told his house was a long two miles off. We then asked for Mr. Strickland's, only to receive the reply that he lived a day's journey farther on. It seemed as if there would be no alternative but a lodging under the stars, when a woman's kindly hand was laid on my arm, and I was led into the house by the mistress of the little inn. Mrs. McFadden had been listening to our inquiries, and the name Stewarts and Strickland attracting her attention, had induced her to make an effort on our behalf. The kind woman put me in a chair by the blazing log fire, and giving directions to a stout Irish girl to bring some warm water and attend to my wet feet, she mixed a hot drink and insisted upon my taking it. The warmth was most grateful, and while I was being thus cared for I could look about me.

"Truly the scene was a novel one. The light from the fire illuminated the room, showing every available space occupied almost to the very verge of the hearth. Men, women and children were sleeping on improvised beds, bundles of all sizes and shapes forming pillows for their shaggy heads. Some lay on the long dresser, some on the bare floor beneath it—all sleeping the sleep of the weary.

"As soon as she saw I was warm and more comfortable, my hostess showed me to the only place in the house that they had to give us. It was a tiny dormitory, more like a birdcage than anything else. The walls were lathed, but without plaster, and both air and light were freely admitted. However, it had a clean bed in it, and I was glad to lie down and watch the river dancing in the moonlight and listen to the rush of the rapids until I fell asleep.

"The following morning a message was sent to my brother to let him know of our arrival, and that evening he ran the rapids in his canoe, and we met again after seven long years of separation."

Mrs. Traill remained in Peterborough with their kind friends, Mr. Stewart and his family, while her husband returned with Mr. Strickland to his clearing on the shores of Lake Katchewanook, the first of the chain of lakes of which the Otonabee is the outlet. Mr. Strickland had taken up land there for the many advantages the locality offered. There was good soil, fine timber, excellent waterpower, rich mineral deposits, and the probability or remote certainty that at some future date the lakes would be connected by canals, the river made navigable by the construction of locks, and a water highway be obtained from Lake Huron *via* Lake Simcoe to the Bay of Quinte and the St. Lawrence, an expectation which appears about to have the first steps taken towards its accomplishment.

Mr. Traill drew his Government grant of land in the neighborhood, the principal portion being in Verulam township, the smaller in Douro, and by the purchase of an additional grant, secured a water frontage. Until he could build a house they lived with Mr. Strickland, during which time Mrs. Traill became initiated into the ways of life in the bush. In her "Backwoods of Canada," there is a very pretty description of these first few months of life in Canada, and of her acquaintance with the natural history surrounding her new home.

On the 11th of December, 1833, they moved into the new house, which was duly named "Westove." Here they lived seven happy years, for though they had to endure all the hardships and trials inseparable from the early settlement of the bush, they yet were busy and hopeful, happy in the society of each other and the neighborhood of her brother and his family. Mr. Moodie had also moved up from his first location near Cobourg, in February, 1834, and bought land on the Douro side of the lake, about a mile beyond Mr. Strickland's homestead.

The erection of a good sawmill and a bridge over the river also gave them readier access to a market at Peterborough and to their friends, and tended to lessen the loneliness of the situation. They all had suffered at times from the low fever and ague, and the various vicissitudes of farm life, but were always ready to help each other or their less fortunate neighbors.

In 1835, Mrs. Traill again took up her pen. The "Backwoods of Canada" was written, and in 1836 was published in London by Charles Knight, Ludgate Street, for the "Library of Entertaining Knowledge" Series. This volume contained much valuable information for intending emigrants, and had a wide circulation. Though all the hardships and discomforts of life in the bush were told with graphic fidelity, they were described with a cheerful and optimistic pen, as of one who had a far-seeing eye into the future capabilities of the country and a present knowledge of its boundless resources and value, so that the picture of the rough life did not deter many from venturing to embark their all in the effort to make a better home for themselves and their children in the New World, but rather the reverse. The author's cheerful, happy spirit robbed the backwoods of its terrors.

When the rebellion of 1837 broke out, Mr. Traill—as did every other half-pay officer in the clearing—hastened to offer his services to the Government.

"The tidings of the rising was brought to our clearing from Peterborough," writes Mrs. Traill, "the messenger arriving at midnight through the snow to call all loyal men to the defence of their country. No time was lost that night, and before dawn I said farewell to my husband. The next day my maid left me—she had a lover and must go and keep him from going to the wars—then the manservant had to follow and see about his people; so there I was alone in the bush with three small children, the eldest scarcely four years old. Jamie and I had to roll in the logs for the fire. He was the cleverer of the two, for he tied a rope to the log, and with his baby help I managed to keep the fires going until a neighbor came to help us."

Mr. Traill, however, only went as far as Cobourg, for by the time the men there were enrolled, orders countermanding their march came from Toronto, and, after some weeks of vexatious delay and uncertainty, they were disbanded and returned to their homes. Mr. Moodie had, however, gone direct to Toronto, and, being commissioned in one of the regiments serving on the Niagara frontier, his return was delayed for months. During this long winter Mrs. Traill was often with her sister, and Mr. Moodie, in several of his letters speaks most gratefully of their kindness to his wife.

In the sketch, "The First Death in the Clearing," Mrs. Traill gives an instance of how she was called upon to go to the bedside of sorrow or sickness, and reading between the lines one can see what a comfort her loving sympathy must have been to the bereaved mother. Jessie is still alive and often visits Mrs. Traill, bringing her kindly offerings of fresh eggs and butter from the farm. Last summer when Mrs. Traill was so ill that few thought she would recover, Jessie's grief was great. She recalled over and over again the kindness to her in the bush in those early days. "Ay, an' she was sae bonnie; sic a bonnie leddy, wi' her pink cheeks an' her blue e'en, an' she was sae lovin' and dear; my, but I'll greet sair if she is ta'en away!" But Jessie's prayers for the recovery of the dear old friend were answered, and we have her with us still.

In 1839, Mr. Traill sold the farm on the lake, and bought a house and lot in what was lately known as Ashburnham, now a part of Peterborough, where they lived until 1846, when they removed to Rice Lake, and subsequently purchased "Oaklands."

Meanwhile Mrs. Traill had not been idle. They were very poor, as all settlers of Mr. Traill's class and education were in those days, unfitted for the rough life and to cope with the difficulties which the work entailed, and his wife's pen was frequently the means of keeping the wolf from the door. She wrote many short stories and sketches for the magazines both in England and the States, the *Anglo American* being one of those in the latter country; and, in 1850, "Lady Mary and her Nurse," more familiar to present-day readers as "Afar in the Forest," was published. In this little volume there is a story of the grey squirrels, that used to be the delight of my early childhood.

The Traills had removed from Ashburnham to "Wolf Tower," a house belonging to Mr. Bridges, which attained some celebrity; from there they went to live in a small log-house on a rise called Mount Ararat, above a deep ravine on the shores of Rice Lake, and it was here, among the actual surroundings, so well depicted on its pages, that Mrs. Traill wrote "The Canadian Crusoes." It was published by Messrs. Hall & Vertue, London, and later the copyright of both it and "Lady Mary and her Nurse" were bought by Messrs. Nelson & Sons, Edinburgh. These books have gone through many editions and been issued under more than one title, given them by the publisher, but the authoress has not received any further remuneration than the £50 paid for the copyright. They are now on sale in every bookshop as "Lost in the Backwoods" and "Afar in the Forest."

After the purchase and removal to "Oaklands," "A Guide for the Female Emigrant" was written and published in London. Owing to some mismanagement of her editor and the publisher, the authoress received very small return for this useful book.

Mrs. Traill's family now numbered nine, four sons and five daughters (of whom only two sons and two daughters survive), yet, with all the cares and anxiety, as well as the necessary work which the bringing up of a young family entailed, added to the hard labor of farm life, her love of flowers and for natural history in general was a continual source of pleasure and eventually of profit. She lost no opportunity of studying the botany of the country, and was ever seeking for new specimens to add to her herbarium or collection of dried flowers, ferns, and mosses, and making notes of the locality and conditions of their growth. This is still one of her chief pleasures and occupations; she has the gleanings of last summer now ready to put down during the coming winter months.

On the 26th of August, 1857, owing to some cause of accident never ascertained, the crowning misfortune of all the losses in the bush happened. They were burnt out and lost absolutely everything—all the treasures they had striven so hard to save, books, manuscripts and other valuables, the family barely escaping with their lives. Mr. Traill felt the loss very much, especially of his books. He never quite recovered the shock and sorrow of seeing his family thrown thus homeless on the world. Their eldest son was married; the youngest was only a child of ten years. Mr. Strickland and other friends were most kind, helpful and sympathetic, but the loss could never be recovered.

They stayed for some time with Mrs. Traill's brother, Mr. Strickland, and then removed to a house placed at their service by their friend Mrs. Stewart, where Mr. Traill died, after a short but severe illness.

Upon her husband's death, Mr. Strickland urged Mrs. Traill to return to the old neighborhood of their first settlement, now a thriving village, and her daughter Mary obtaining a position as teacher in the school there, they returned to live once more on the banks of the Otonabee. Mrs. Traill had several times during these years sent home small collections of pressed

ferns and mosses. These found a ready sale in England. One of these collections attracted the attention of Lady Charlotte Greville, who succeeded in so interesting Lord Palmerston in Mrs. Traill's literary work as to
obtain for her a grant of £100 from a special fund.

With this unexpected and welcome present Mrs. Traill purchased the
house and lot where she now lives, and which with a loving thought of her
husband's old home in the Orkneys and of their first home in the bush,
she has called "Westove."

Lady Charlotte Greville also sent her a large package of seeds and a
screw press, with which she could press her ferns more effectually.

In 1869, her botanical notes were utilized in supplying the letterpress
for her niece, Mrs. FitzGibbon's "Canadian Wild Flowers," and in 1884,
Mrs. Traill published her "Studies of Plant Life in Canada," also illustrated by her niece, now Mrs. Chamberlin.

While the latter book was in the press, Mrs. Traill paid a visit to Ottawa
and enjoyed the pleasure of meeting many who had been interested in her
work, of renewing old friendships and making the personal acquaintance
of many with whom she had corresponded on kindred subjects. She was
also greatly indebted to Mr. James Fletcher, of the Experimental Farm,
for his kind aid in reading the proofs of her book.

Mrs. Traill went to Government House, and took a lively interest in the
gay scenes on the skating rink and toboggan slides, as smiling and happy as the youngest among us, and winning admiration and affection from
all those who had the pleasure of seeing her. It was during this visit to
Ottawa that the photograph was taken from which the engraving forming
the frontispiece to the present volume is made. Mrs. Traill was then in her
eighty-fourth year.

The facsimile engraving shown on the page facing this portrait of Mrs.
Traill is taken from part of a letter written recently to a friend whom she
values highly. It is interesting not only as a specimen of the handwriting
of one of such advanced years, but also as indicating the unaffected piety
of her life.

"Studies of Plant Life" is now a rare book, chance copies selling for
three times the original price.

Mrs. Traill had always received kindly presents from her sisters in England, and during the last few years of their lives they were in a better posi-

tion to help her and add to the comforts of her home surroundings. The copyright of the "Queens of England," left her by her sister Agnes, although sold for half its value, has added a little to her very small income.

In 1893, hearing of the likelihood of the sale of the little island in Stony Lake, where a poor Indian girl was buried, Mrs. Traill wrote to the Department at Ottawa to ask that it should be granted her. It was but a tiny island, and her anxiety to preserve the Indian girl's grave from desecration induced her to take this step. Mr. Sandford Fleming kindly interested himself in her behalf, and the request was granted.

Detail of a "Letter from Catharine Parr Traill," from *Pearls and Pebbles* (1894).

The following extract from her old friend's announcement is so gratifying to Mrs. Traill that I cannot refrain from quoting it:

"I have the pleasure to inform you that by the same post you will receive a patent for 'Polly Cow's Island,' in the river Otonabee, township of Douro.

"It has been a great pleasure to everyone here, from the highest to the lowest official, to do everything in their power to do you honorable service and gratify your every wish—every one of them feeling that the most

"Polly Cow's Island," from *Pearls and Pebbles* (1894).

any of them can do is but the smallest acknowledgment which is due to you for your life-long devotion to Canada."

The patent is beautifully engrossed by hand and is highly valued by the owner.

Another honor paid Mrs. Traill was the compliment of calling a remarkable form of the fern *Aspidium marginale*, which she found growing near the village of Lakefield, on a vacant town lot that was only partially cleared from the forest trees, Mrs. Traill's Shield Fern—*A. marginale* (Swz.) var: Traillæ—is not the least valued by her.

There have been many events in Mrs. Traill's life not mentioned in this brief biographical introduction to her book, such as bereavements, in the death of two of her sons and her daughter Mary—trials patiently borne and sorrows suffered that had overwhelmed her but for her trust in Providence and her unfailing reliance on his will. I have passed them by, not because they are without interest, but because it would be turning back a cloud of sorrow to dim the dear old eyes with tears, and hide for awhile the silver lining that has glorified her life.

She has given such pretty glimpses of her home by the Otonabee, in the sketches, that I should only spoil it were I to attempt to describe it in greater detail. Anyone seeing her now in the pretty sittingroom, busy with her gay patchwork, stitching away at quilts for the Indian Missionary Auxiliary basket, or putting down the ferns and mosses gathered last summer during her visit to the island of Minnewawa, and watching the light in her blue eyes, the smile on her soft old face, unwrinkled by a frown, or listening to her clever conversation, sparkling with well-told anecdotes and incidents of men and things garnered during her long life and retained with a memory that is phenomenal, would realize that the secret of her peaceful old age, her unclouded intellect, and the brightness of her eye, is due to her trust in Providence, her contentment with her lot, and a firm belief in the future where a happy reunion with the loved ones awaits her.

The following lines, written on her mother's eightieth birthday by Mrs. Traill's third daughter, Mary (the late Mrs. Muchall), though faulty in metre, are so descriptive that I cannot end my brief sketch better than by quoting them:

"Eighty to-day is our mother,
　　A picture so peaceful and fair,
The lilies of fourscore summers
　　Asleep in her silvered hair.

"Eighty to-day, yet the love-light
　　Shines as soft in her sweet blue eyes,
As touched with a ray from heaven
　　Of the peace that never dies.

"The happy spirit of childhood,
　　That with some is too quickly past,
Caught by some magic enchantment,
　　Is flooding her life to the last.

"Eighty to-day, and her children,
        Near or far in a distant land,
    Are strong sons and happy daughters,
        A loved and a loving band.

"In our hearts she'll live forever;
        When she leaves for a world more fair,
    Her smile will be still more radiant
        As she welcomes each dear one there."

CATHARINE PARR TRAILL: A LIST OF IMPORTANT DATES

1802 Born in Rotherhyde Parish, England, 5th of 8 children: Elizabeth, Agnes, Sara, Jane, Catharine, Susanna, Samuel, Thomas. Parents: Thomas and Elizabeth Strickland.

1803 Family moves to Stowe House, Suffolk.

1804 Family moves to Reydon Hall, Suffolk.

1818 Death of father—Thomas Strickland.
Publication of *The Tell Tale: An Original Collection of Moral and Amusing Stories*.

1819 Publication of *Disobedience; or, Mind What Mama Says*; and *Reformation; or, The Cousins*.

1821 Publication of *Nursery Fables*.

1822 Publication of *Little Downy; or, The History of a Field Mouse: A Moral Tale*.

1825 Publication of *The Flower-Basket; or, Poetical Blossoms: Original Nursery Rhymes and Tales*.

1826 Publication of *Prejudice Reproved; or, The History of the Negro Toy-Seller*; and *The Young Emigrants; or, Pictures of Life in Canada*.

1827 Publication of *The Juvenile Forget-Me-Not; or, Cabinet of Entertainment and Instruction*.

1828 Publication of *The Keepsake Guineas; or, The Best Use of Money*; and *Amendment; or, Charles Grant and His Sister*.

1829 Engaged to Francis Harral.

1820s Contributions to English periodicals.

1830   Publication of *Sketches from Nature; or, Hints to Juvenile Naturalists*.

1831   Publication of *Sketch Book of a Young Naturalist; or, Hints to the Students of Nature*; and *Narratives of Nature, and History Book for Young Naturalists*.
Engagement with Francis Harral ended.

1832   Marries Thomas Traill (May 13).
Moves to Douro, Upper Canada (departs July 7).

1833   Birth of James George.

1836   Publication of *The Backwoods of Canada*.
Birth of Katherine Agnes.

1837   Birth of Thomas Henry.

1838   Birth of Anne Fotheringham[e].

1839   Family moves to Rice Lake.

1840   Birth of Mary Ellen Bridges.

1841   Birth of Mary Elizabeth Jane.
Death of Mary Ellen.

1843   Birth of Eleanor Stewart (died an infant).

1844   Birth of William Edward.

1847   Family moves to Gore's Landing.

1848   Birth of Walter John.

1849   Family moves to Hamilton Township.

1830s, Publishing in English, Scottish, Canadian, and American
1840s   periodicals, such as *Chambers's Edinburgh Journal*, *Literary*
and   *Garland*, *Sharpe's London Journal*, *Anglo American Magazine*.
1850s

1852   Publication of *Canadian Crusoes: A Tale of the Rice Lake Plains*.

1854   Publication of *The Canadian Settler's Guide* (or *The Female Emigrant's Guide*).

1856   Publication of *Lady Mary and Her Nurse*.

1859   Death of Thomas Traill.

1860   Catharine moves to Lakefield, "Westove."

1868   Publication of *Canadian Wild Flowers*, together with Agnes FitzGibbon.

1885   Publication of *Studies of Plant Life in Canada*.

1893   Given Polly Cow Island in Lake Katchewanook.

1894   Publication of *Pearls and Pebbles*.

1895   Publication of *Cot and Cradle Stories*.

1899   Death of Catharine Parr Traill.

THE STRICKLAND FAMILY TREE

Susanna Bott(1) = Thomas Strickland = (2) Elizabeth Homer
d.c. 1790; no issue   (1758–1818)   (1722–1864)

    Elizabeth (Eliza)
    1794–1875

    Agnes
    1796–1874

    Sarah   =   (1) Robert Childs   (2) Richard Gwillym
    1798–1890   d.1839   d.1868

    Jane Margaret
    1800–1888

    Catharine Parr = **Thomas Traill**
    1802–1899   1793–1859

    Susanna   =   J.W.D. Moodie
    1803–1885   1797–1869

    Samuel   = (1) Emma Black
    1805–1867   d.1826
                         (2) Mary Reid
                              1808–1850
                         (3) Katherine Blackburn
                              d.1890

    Thomas   =   Margaretta A. Thompson
    1807–1874   d.1863

THE TRAILL

Anne Fotheringhame (1) = Thomas Traill
d. 1828   (1793–1859)

Walter
1815–1845

John Heddle
1819–1847
m.
Eliza Dunbar
d. 1844)

James
George
1833–1867
m.
Amelia Keye
Muchall

Katherine
Agness
Strickland
(Kate)
1863–1922

Thomas Henry
Strickland
(Harry)
1837–1870
m.
Lilas Grant
Maclean

Francis
(Frank)
(b.c.1842)

Henrietta
Anna
b.1841

William
Henry
1843–1902

Richard
Henry
1857–1940

Thomas
Edward
Strickland
1859–1931

Catherine
Amelia
1861–1862

Agness
Strickland
b. 1863
d. infant

George
Frederick
b. 1863
d. infant

George
Herbert
b. 1866

Charles Henry
Strickland
1865–1949

Katharine
Parr
(Katie)
b. 1867

George
James
McManus
1869–1950

FAMILY TREE

= (2) Catharine Parr Strickland
    (1802–1899)

Anne Traill Fotheringhame (Annie) 1838–1931 m. James Parr Clinton Atwood 1836–1912	Mary Ellen Bridges 1840–1841	Mary Elizabeth Jane 1841–1892 m. Thomas W. Mitchell d. 1898	Eleanor Stewart 1843 d. infant	William Edward 1844–1917 m. Hariette McKay 1847–1920	Walter John Strickland 1848–1932 m. Mary E. Purdy
— Henry Arthur Strickland 1860–1864		— Hargrave Henry b. 1865		— Walter 1870–1932	— Walter Archibald Strickland 1882–1883
— Emily Grace 1863–1940		— Evelyn Mary b. 1867		— Katherine Barbara 1871–1918	— Cora Gilbert
— Clinton Arthur Strickland 1865–1952		— Caroline Gwillym 1871–1896		— William McKay b. 1875	— Hordesty Gilbert
— Katharine Stewart 1868–1954		— Norman Stewart 1873–1892		— Henry 1877–1878	
— George Evan 1869–1964				— Ethel b. 1879	
— Anne Traill Fotheringhame 1871–1972				— Jessie b. 1881	
— Florence Marion 1874–1957				— Mary b. 1883	
				— Maria b. 1884	
				— Harriett b. 1888	
				— Annie b. 1892	

"Catharine Traill in 1867."

ENDNOTES

EDITOR'S INTRODUCTION

1 See the Traill Family Papers in the National Archives of Canada.
2 See Mary Agnes FitzGibbon's biographical sketch in Appendix A; see also the Traill Family Papers.
3 Appendix A.
4 *A Trip to Manitoba* (1880) is one of Mary Agnes FitzGibbon's published works.
5 See the Traill Family Papers.
6 See the *Anglo American Magazine* for a series of articles on Canada.

PLEASANT DAYS OF MY CHILDHOOD

1 Samuel Woodworth (1785-1842), "The Old Oaken Bucket," stanza 1; first titled "The Bucket," collected in his *Melodies, Duets, Songs, and Ballads* (1826), and set to music by Frederick Smith.
2 Oliver Goldsmith (1728-1774), *The Traveller; or, A Prospect of Society* (1764), line 72.
3 Job 14:2.
4 Thomas à Kempis (1380-1471), *Imitation of Christ* (c. 1420), Book 1, chapter 3: "So passes away the glory of this world."
5 Oliver Goldsmith (1728-1774), *The Deserted Village* (1770), line 137: "Near yonder copse, where once the garden smiled."
6 This is a very early Canadian poem by Traill, dated 1839 in the Traill Family Papers (National Archives of Canada). It was previously published in a number of different places: see the *Literary Garland* n.s. 4 (May 1846): 213; *Anglo American Magazine* 7.3 (September 1855): 238; *The Canadian Monthly and National Review* 1.1 (1872): 532-3; also *Vicks Monthly Magazine* 8 (May 1885): 131.

SUNSET AND SUNRISE ON LAKE ONTARIO

1   William Wilfr[e]d Campbell (1858-1918), "Ode to the Lakes (In June)," Stanza 3,
    from *Lake Lyrics and Other Poems* (1889)
2   John Milton (1608-1674), *Paradise Lost* (1674), Book XII, line 646:
    The world was all before them, where to choose
    Their place of rest, and Providence their guide:
    They, hand in hand, with wand'ring steps and slow,
    Through Eden took their solitary way.
    These are the closing lines of *Paradise Lost*, as Adam and Eve leave the Garden of
    Eden.
3   Latin for the end of the world, the most northern part of the world, or the outermost
    known limits.
4   Thomas Campbell (1777-1844), *Pleasures of Hope* (1799), Part 1, line 7: "'Tis distance
    lends enchantment to the view / And robes the mountain in its azure hue."
5   Psalms 19:1.
6   For similar phrasing, see John Keats (1795-1821). "On First Looking into Chapman's
    Homer" (1816): "Then felt I like some watcher of the skies."

MEMORIES OF A MAY MORNING

1   George Herbert (1593-1633), "Virtue" in *The Temple* (1633), Stanza 1.
2   Henry Wadsworth Longfellow (1807-1882), "The Poet and His Songs," from *Ultima
    Thule* (1880), Stanza 1: "As the birds come in the spring, / We know not from where..."
3   Henry Wadsworth Longfellow, *Evangeline* (1847), Part 1, Section 3:
    Silently one by one, in the
        infinite meadows of heaven
    Blossomed the lovely stars, the
        forget-me-nots of the angels.
4   Henry Wadsworth Longfellow, "The Day is Done," from *The Belfry of Bruges and
    Other Poems* (1846), Stanza 11:
    And the night shall be filled with music,
        And the cares that infest the day,
    Shall fold their tents, like the Arabs,
        And as silently steal away.
    This particular paragraph reveals Traill's appreciation of Longfellow; she often appro-
    priates his imagery without acknowledging her source.
5   Robert Burns (1759-1796), "To a Mouse" (1785), Stanza 7.
6   William Shakespeare, *The Tempest*, Act 4, Scene 1:
    Our revels now are ended These our actors,
    As I foretold you, were all spirits and
    Are melted into air, into thin air;

And, like the baseless fabric of this vision,

The cloud-capped towers, the gorgeous palaces,

The solemn temples, the great globe itself,

Yea, all which it inherit, shall dissolve;

And, like this insubstantial pageant faded,

Leave not a rack behind. We are such atuff

As dreams are made on...

7   Charles Dickens (1812-1870), *Barnaby Rudge* (1841), Chapter 6: "'Keep up your
spirits! Never say die! Bow, wow, wow! I'm a devil, I'm a devil, I'm a devil!'"; also
R.H. Barham (1785-1845), *The Merchant of Venice* (a parody):

With a wink of his eye, his friend made reply,

In his jocular manner, sly, caustic, and dry,

"Still the same boy, Bassanio—never say 'die'!"

ANOTHER MAY MORNING

1   William Wordsworth (1770-1850), "Lines Written in Early Spring," stanza 4-5, in
Lyrical Ballads (1798).

2   Traill's footnote refers to Thomas McIlwraith (1824-1903), *The Birds of Ontario*
(1886), 195.

3   Jane Roscoe (1797-1853), author of religious poetry and hymns; her work includes
Poems by one of the Authors of Poems for Youth by a Family Circle (1820) and *Poems*
(1843).

4   Isaiah 11:9.

5   John Keats (1795-1821), *Endymion* (1818), Book I, line 1:

A thing of beauty is a joy forever:

Its loveliness increases; it will never

Pass into nothingness; but still will keep

A bower quiet for us, and a sleep

Full of sweet dreams, and health, and quiet breathing.

6   Henry Wadsworth Longfellow, "The Builders," in *The Seaside and the Fireside*
(1849), stanza 1-4:

All are architects of Fate,

  Working in these walls of Time;

Some with massive deeds and great,

  Some with ornaments of rhyme.

Nothing useless is, or low;

  Everything in its place is best;

And what seems but idle show,

  Strengthens and supports the rest.

> For the structure that we raise,
> Time is with materials filled;
> Our todays and yesterdays
> Are the blocks with which we build.
>
> Truly shape and fashion these;
> Leave no yawning gaps between;
> Think not, because no man sees,
> Such things will remain unseen.

7   The source for this quotation has not been found.

8   John Donne (1572-1631), *Epithalamion on the Lady Elizabeth and Count Palatine* (ca. 1613), Stanza 1.

9   English Proverb, ca. 1555.

10 Emily Taylor (1795-1872), "A Mother's Love," stanza 7:

> There are teachings on earth, and sky, and air,
>
> The heavens the glory of God declare!
>
> But louder than the voice beneath, above,
>
> He is heard to speak through a mother's love.

Found in *Third Book of Reading Lessons* (1869), in the *Canadian Series of School Books*. See also Psalms 19:1: "The heavens declare the glory of God, and the firmament sheweth his handywork."

11 See Matthew 6: 26-29; and Luke 12: 24-27.

MORE ABOUT MY FEATHERED FRIENDS

1   Charles Pelham Mulvaney (1835-1885), a Canadian poet. See his *Lyrics, Songs and Sonnets* (1880). The source of this particular poem has not been found.

2   See Henry Wadsworth Longfellow, "The Day is Done" (1846), stanza 11.

3   Alexander Wilson (1766-1813), *American Ornithology* (1808-1813).

4   Alexander Wilson, *American Ornithology*, found in Volume 2, page 175, of the 1831 edition. Cited by Thomas McIlwraith (1824-1903) in *The Birds of Ontario* (1886), 324:

> When all the gay scenes of the summer are o'er,
>
> And autumn slow enters so silent and sallow,
>
> And millions of warblers which charmed us before
>
> Have fled in the train of the sun-seeking Swallow.
>
> The Bluebird forsaken, yet true to its home,
>
> Still lingers and looks for a milder to-morrow,
>
> Till forced by the [rigors] of winter to roam,
>
> It sings its adieu in a lone note of sorrow.

5   If a man is said not to know the difference between meum and tuum, it is a polite (colloquial) way of saying he is a thief.

6 See Frances Stewart (1794-1872) *Our Forest Home* (1902). The Stewarts were close friends of the Traills, sharing many similar interests and a common upper middle-class background.

7 Nursery rhyme:

> The fox and his wife, without any strife,
>
> Said they never ate a better goose in all their life:
>
> They did very well without fork or knife,
>
> And the little ones picked the bones O!

8 See McIlwraith, *Birds of Ontario* (1886), page 195; the Yellow-headed Blackbird is labelled "Genus Xanthocephalus Bonaparte." "Xanthocephalus" means "yellow-headed."

9 Alexander Wilson, "The Fisherman's Hymn" in *American Ornithology*; see Volume 1, page 50 of the 1831 edition:

> She rears her young on yonder tree
>
> She leaves her faithful mate to mind 'em;
>
> Like us, for fish she sails to sea,
>
> And, plunging, shows us where to find 'em.
>
> Yo, ho, my hearts! let's seek the deep,
>
> Ply every ear, and cheerly wish her,
>
> While slow the bending net we sweep,
>
> God bless the fish-hawk and the fisher.

10 Proverb: "All is fish that comes to my net," or "All is fish that cometh to net."

THE ENGLISH SPARROW: A DEFENSE

1 William Shakespeare, *As You Like It*, Act 2, Scene 3, line 43-5.

2 The so-called "Sparrow War" refers to the debate over the merits and demerits of the introduction of the English house sparrow to North America in the winter of 1850-1851 by Nicolas Pike, director of the Brooklyn Institute.

3 Daniel Fenning, *The Universal Spelling-book; or, a new and easy guide to the English language* (1767). In "Life truly painted, in the natural History of Tommy and Harry," naughty boy Harry is known for the phrase, "I don't care." Harry meets an unfortunate end, and "*don't care* was his Ruin at last."

4 Matthew 10:29.

5 1 Corinthians 9:9: "For it is written in the law of Moses, Thou shalt not muzzle the mouth of the ox that treadeth out the corn. Doth God take care for oxen?"

6 Alexander Pope (1688-1744), *An Essay On Man* (1733), Epistle 1, lines 85-88.

7 Sparrow introduced by Nicolas Pike, Director of the Brooklyn Institute, 1877-78.

8 Luke 10:5.

9 Proverb, c. 1534.

10 Proverb: "Give a dog a bad name and hang him."

11 The speaker has not been identified.

NOTES FROM MY OLD DIARY

1   Anne Letitia Barbauld (1743-1825), "To Mrs. P___, with some Drawings of Birds and Insects," in *Poems* (1773). There is a misprint in Traill's quotation; the final line should read "lively crimson."

2   A banshee is the domestic spirit of certain Irish or Highland Scottish families, supposed to take an interest in the welfare of the family—and to wait at the death of one of the family.

3   George Friedrich Handel (1685-1759), *Messiah* (1741), Part 3, Number 44, Duet (alto and tenor: based on 1 Corinthians 15:55-56.

4   The Ottawa Field-Naturalists' Club. Traill's niece, Agnes (Moodie) FitzGibbon Chamberlin (1833-1913) was active in the club, founded in 1879.

5   Isaac Newton (1642-1727); see his *Opticks* (1704) or *Philosophiae naturalis principia mathematica* (1678).

THE SPIDER

1   Proverbs 30:28,

2   Henry Wadsworth Longfellow, "A Psalm of Life," in *Voices of the Night* (1839), stanza 9:

> Let us, then, be up and doing,
> With a heart for any fate;
> Still achieving, still pursuing
> Learn to labor and to wait.

3   Caroline Anne Bowles Southey (1786-1854), "The Reed-Sparrow's Nest" (1829), in *The New Year's Gift; and Juvenile Souvenir* (1829), ed. Mrs. Alaric Watts: 'Twas an instinct unerring (God's gift to the weak) / Taught the poor little builder this covert to seek."

PROSPECTING, AND WHAT I FOUND IN MY DIGGING

1   Shakespeare, *The Merchant of Venice*, Act 2, scene 7, line 65.

THE ROBIN AND THE MIRROR

1   A Wardian case is a box or frame with glass sides and top, used for transporting or growing delicate plants; invented by Nathaniel B. Ward.

IN THE CANADIAN WOODS

1   Henry Wadsworth Longfellow, "Sunrise on the Hills" in *Voices of the Night* (1839), lines 31-36.

2   The source has not been found. For similar phrasing, see William Wordsworth (1770-1850), "I Wandered Lonely as a Cloud" (1807):

> A host, of golden daffodils;
>
> Beside the lake, beneath the trees,
>
> Fluttering and dancing in the breeze.

3   William Cullen Bryant (1794-1878), "A Forest Hymn" (1825), found in *The Poetical Works of William Cullen Bryant* (1883), Volume 1.

4   For similar sentiments, see William Cullen Bryant, "The Disinterred Warrior" (1827), in *The Poetical Works of William Cullen Bryant* (1883):

> A noble race! but they are gone,
>
>   With their old forests wide and deep,
>
> And we have built our homes upon
>
>   Fields where their generations sleep.

5   Isaiah 41:12: "Thou shalt seek them, and shalt not find them, even them that contended with thee;" Job 7:21: "... for now shall I sleep in the dust; and thou shalt seek me in the morning, but I shall not be."

6   William Shakespeare, *As You Like It*, Act 2, scene 5, lines 1-7.

7   An old meaning of pensioner is someone who accepts charitable support.

8   Matthew 6:26-28: "Behold the fowls of the air: for they sow not, neither do they reap, nor gather into barns... Consider the lilies of the field, how they grow; they toil not, neither do they spin."

9   Acts 7:49-50: "Heaven is my throne, and earth is my footstool: what house will ye build me? saith the Lord: or what is the place of rest? / Hath not my hand made all these things?"

10 Anglican Morning Prayer service, "Benedicte, omnia opera": "O ye Winds of God, bless ye the Lord: praise him, and magnify him for ever."

11 See, for example, Henry Wadsworth Longfellow, "The Builders," stanza 4, from *The Seaside and the Fireside* (1849): "Think not, because no man sees, / Such things will remain unseen." See also William Cullen Bryant, "A Forest Hymn" (1825), in *The Poetical Works of William Cullen Bryant* (1883):

> Thou hast not left
>
> Thyself without a witness, in the shades,
>
> Of thy perfections. Grandeur, strength, and grace
>
> Are here to speak of thee.

12 The source for this quotation has not been found, but varients appear elsewhere in Traill's work. See *Canadian Settler's Guide* (1854): "Like joys that linger as they fall, / Whose last are dearest;" see also *Canadian Wild Flowers* (1868): "Bright flowers that linger as they fall, / Whose last are dearest;" and *Studies of Plant Life in Canada* (1885):

> Tall fairer flowers are all decayed,
>
>   And thou appearest;

> Like joys that linger as they fade,
> Whose last are dearest.

13   Alexander McLachlan (1818-1896), "October," found in *The Poetical Works of Alexander McLachlan* (1900), 3rd stanza.

14   Richard Brathwaite (1588-1673), *English Gentleman* (1630): "Time and tide stayeth for no man."

15   Lord Byron (1788-1824), *Childe Harold'sPilgrimage. A Romance* (1812), Canto 2, stanza 25:

> To sit on rocks, to muse o'er flood and fell,
> To slowly trace the forest's shady scene,
> Where things that own not man's dominion dwell,
> And mortal foot hath ne'er, or rarely been;
> To climb the trackless mountain all unseen,
> With the wild flock that never needs a fold;
> Alone o'er steeps and foaming falls to lean;
> This is not solitude; 'tis but to hold
> Converse with Nature's charms, and view her stores unroll'd.

16   Exodus 16:18: "And when they did mete it with an omer, he that gathered much had nothing over, and he that gathered little had no lack; they gathered every man according to his eating."

17   From a traditional nursery rhyme; see James Reeves, "Flowers and Frost," from *The Faber Book of Nursery Verse* (1958):

> Flowers are yellow
> And flowers are red;
> Frost is white
> As an old man's head.
> Daffodil, foxglove,
> Rose, sweet pea -
> Flowers and frost
> Can never agree.
> Flowers will wither
> And summer's lost
> When over the mountain
> Comes King Frost.

18   Popular meaning, "inglorious." See 1 Samuel 4:21-22:

> And she named the child Ichabod, saying, The glory is departed from Israel: because the ark of God was taken, and because of her father in law and her husband. / And she said, The glory is departed from Israel: for the ark of God is taken.

19   Susanna Moodie (1803-1885), "Indian Summer," in *Life in the Clearings* (1853).

20   The source of this quotation is unknown.

21 "Flowers and Frost," stanza 2:
    White are the fields
    Where King Frost reigns;
    And the ferns he draws
    On window-panes,
    White and stiff
    Are their curling fronds.
    White are the hedges
    And stiff the ponds.
    So cruel and hard
    Is winter's King,
    With his icy breath
    On everything.

22 Decca is a region in India.

23 2 Corinthians 5:17: "Therefore if any man be in Christ, he is a new creature: old things are passed away; behold, all things are become new."

24 Genesis 8:22: "While the earth remaineth, seed-time and harvest, and cold and heat, and summer and winter, and day and night shall not cease."

25 Malachi 3:6: "For I am the Lord; I change not; therefore ye sons of Jacob are not consumed."

26 Poem by Traill, previously published in *Canadian Monthly and National Review* (March 1872): 238; called "A Song for the Sleigh" in the Traill Family Papers (National Archives of Canada) and dated 1836.

THE FIRST DEATH IN THE CLEARING

1 Published as "The Bereavement," in the *Literary Garland* n.s. 4 (1846): 69-72.

2 Henry Wadsworth Longfellow, "Resignation," in *The Seaside and The Fireside* (1849), stanza 1.

3 Sir Walter Scott (1771-1832), *Marmion* (1808): "He stayed not for brake and he stopped not for stone, / He swam the Eske river when ford there was none."

4 Agnes Strickland (1796-1874), "The Infant," in *The Seven Ages of Woman, and Other Poems* (1827): " - stern death was nigh / And life's young wings were fluttering for their flight."

5 Phrase taken from the Anglican Communion Service, general confession: "In new ness of life."

6 Doxology, traditional hymn of praise (1709) by Thomas Ken (1637-1711), in *Morning and Evening Hymns:*.
    Praise God from whom all blessings flow;
    Praise Him all creatures here below;
    Praise him above, ye heavenly host;
    Praise Father, Son, and Holy Ghost.

7   See Agnes Strickland (1796-1874), the last lines of "The Infant," a sonnet published in *The Seven Ages of Woman and Other Poems* (1827), also published in *Victoria Magazine* 1.9 (May 1848): 211, and *The Anglo American Magazine* 2.3 (March 1853): 311. The last line of the poem (which treats of the death of an infant) reads, "Oh! happy child! untried and early blest."

ALONE IN THE FOREST

1   Published as "Female Trials in the Bush," in *Sharpe's London Magazine* 15 (1852): 22-26, and in *Anglo American Magazine* 2 (1852): 426-430.
2   Proverb, English equivalent: "He that grasps at too much, holds nothing fast." (c1205)
3   See Psalms 22:1:
    My God, my God, why hast thou forsaken me? why art thou so far from
    helping me, and from the words of my roaring?
4   A common expression, pejorative, meaning to take without asking permission, referring to French soldiers who invaded and took what they wanted.
5   Shakespeare, *All's Well That Ends Well*, Act 4, scene 4, line 35.

ON THE ISLAND OF MINNEWAWA

1   Thomas Gray (1716-71), "Elegy Written in a Country Churchyard" (1750), stanza 14:
    Full many a gem of purest ray serene,
    The dark unfathomed caves of ocean bear:
    Full many a flower is born to blush unseen,
    And waste its sweetness on the desert air.
2   John Milton (1608-74), *Paradise Lost* (1667), Book 4, lines 675-680.

THE CHILDREN OF THE FOREST

1   Lydia Huntley Sigourney (1791-1865), "Indian Names" (1841), stanza 1, found in *Pocahantas, and Other Poems* (1841).
2   Lares: the spirits of dead ancestors; Penates: the old Latin household gods.
3   Isaiah 55: 7.
4   The source for this quotation has not been found.

THOUGHTS ON VEGETABLE INSTINCT

1   This is one of Traill's constant refrains in this book and elsewhere. For one of her sources, see Thomas Gray (1716-1771), "Elegy Written in a Country Churchyard" (1751): "Full many a flower is born to blush unseen, / And waste its sweetness on the desert air."

2 This is another of Traill's preoccupations. For similar sentiments, see, for example, Longfellow, "The Builders," in *The Seaside and the Fireside* (1849): "Think not, because no man sees, / Such things will remain unseen."

3 Jules Michelet (1798-1874), author of such works as *La Mer* (1861), *Introduction a l'Histoire Universelle* (1835), and *Histoire de France* (1833-1867).

4 See the Traill Family Papers (Public Archives of Canada), Volume 3, 3555:

> What hortus siccus could convey a just portrait of our splendid Nymphoe. My queen of the Lakes defies such a vain attempt at preserving a picture of her charm. The pencil is the only true mirror in which to behold such beauties as hers and other of her aquatic court.

SOME CURIOUS PLANTS

1 Dogbane, also known as Indian Hemp.

SOME VARIETIES OF POLLEN

1 Antoine Laurent de Jussieu (1748-1836).

2 Marcello Malpighi (1628-1694).

3 The mention of Jussieu appears to be an error: this should be John Evelyn (1620-1706), *Silva, or, a disclosure of forest-trees, and the propagation of timber* (1776).

4 The source for the quotation has not been found.

THE CRANBERRY MARSH

1 This refers to a particular type of lacquer.

OUR NATIVE GRASSES

1 Robert Lord Lytton (Owen Meredith) (1831-1891), "The Thistle: Prelude," in *Fables in Song* (1876).

2 Hugh McMillan (1833-1903), *Bible Teachings in Nature* (1866).

3 2 Samuel 21:10:

> And Rizpah the daughter of Aiah took sackcloth, and spread it for her upon the rock, from the beginning of harvest until water dropped upon them out of heaven, and suffered neither the birds of the air to rest on them by day, nor the beasts of the field by night.

4 Previously published in *The Canadian Settler's Guide* (1855).

INDIAN GRASS

1 From Traill's footnote: Samuel Smiles (1812-1904), *Robert Dick, Baker, of Thurso, Geologist and Botanist* (1878).

MOSSES AND LICHENS

1   The source for this quotation has not been found.
2   Mungo Park (1771-1806), *Travels in the Interior Districts of Africa, Performed in the Years 1795, 1796 and 1797. With an account of a subsequent mission to that country in 1805* (first published 1799).
3   1 Corinthians 1: 27-28:
    But God hath chosen the foolish things of the world to confound the wise; and God hath chosen the weak things of the world to confound the things that are mighty;/ And base things of the world, and things which are despised, hath God chosen, yea, and things which are not, to bring to nought things that are.

THE INDIAN MOSS-BAG

1   Traditional lullaby, perhaps inspired by the type of cradle described by Traill.

SOMETHING GATHERS UP THE FRAGMENTS

1   Antoine François de Fourcrois (1755-1809); see his *Elements of Chemistry and Natural History. To which is prefixed, the philosophy of chemistry*, 5th edition (1800).
2   The "economy" of nature was a common eighteenth and nineteenth century expression, popularized by such writers as Carl Linnaeus, in "The Oeconomy of Nature," *Miscellaneous Tracts Relating to Natural History, Husbandry and Physick*, 3rd edition (1775).
3   John 6:12: "…he said unto his disciples, Gather up the fragments that remain, that nothing be lost"
4   Job 38: 11.
5   Alexander Pope (1688-1744), *Essay on Man* (1733), Epistle 1, lines 289-290.
6   Divine Service, Burial of the Dead: "Earth to earth, ashes to ashes, dust to dust; in sure and certain hope of the Resurrection to eternal life, through our Lord Jesus Christ."
7   Psalms 107: 43.

ILLUSTRATION CREDITS

IN THE CANADIAN WOODS

Page 69, Reproduced courtesy John Ross Robertson Collection, Metropolitan Toronto
Reference Library. T 30305.

Page 79, Reproduced courtesy John Ross Robertson Collections, Metropolitan Toronto
Reference Library. T 30301.

THE FIRST DEATH IN THE CLEARING

Page 84, Reproduced courtesy John Ross Robertson Collection, Metropolitan Toronto
Reference Library. T 16440.

ALONE IN THE FOREST

Page 93, Reproduced courtesy Metropolitan Toronto Reference Library. T 14381.

Page 94, Photography by Louisa Yick, University of Toronto Zoology Department.

ON THE ISLAND OF MINNEWAWA

Page 101, Reproduced courtesy Metropolitan Toronto Reference Library. T 13437.

THE CHILDREN OF THE FOREST

Page 105, Reproduced courtesy John Ross Robertson Collection, Metropolitan Toronto
Reference Library. T 16410.

THOUGHTS ON VEGETABLE INSTINCT

Page 110, Reproduced by Thomas Fisher Rare Book Library.

OUR NATIVE GRASSES

Page 127, Reproduced courtesy Metropolitan Toronto Reference Library. T 13438.

INDIAN GRASS

Page 134, Reproduced courtesy John Ross Robertson Collection, Metropolitan Toronto
Reference Library. T 14975.

THE INDIAN MOSS BAG

Page 142, Reproduced by Thomas Fisher Rare Book Library.

APPENDIX A

Page 152, Reproduced by Thomas Fisher Rare Book Library.
Page 155, Reproduced by Thomas Fisher Rare Book Library.
Page 173, Reproduced by Thomas Fisher Rare Book Library.

APPENDIX B

Page 182, Courtesy National Archives of Canada. C 67346.

APPENDIX C

Pages 183–185, Family trees: Adapted from Carl Ballstadt, Elizabeth Hopkins and Michael A. Peterman (eds), *I Bless You In My Heart*. Toronto: University of Toronto Press, 1996.

INDEX

ABOUT THE EDITOR

ELIZABETH THOMPSON is a writer living in Toronto, Ontario. She has taught at the University of Toronto and The University of Western Ontario. Elizabeth has written extensively about early Canadian literature, as well as contemporary Canadian fiction and poetry. Her publications include *The Pioneer Woman: A Canadian Type* (1991), an edition of Susanna Moodie's *Roughing It in the Bush* (1997) and *The Emigrant's Guide to North America* (1998).